My Travels:
Spain
Egypt
Israel
Thailand
China
Brazil
South Africa

Haiti
Greece
Jamaica
Curasoo

St. Thomas
Nasau Bermuda
Aruba

Canada
Alaska
Cuba

Mexico

W9-CNZ-147

SINGING THE LORD'S SONG IN A STRANGE LAND

JOSEPH E. LOWERY

Abingdon Press
Nashville

SINGING THE LORD'S SONG IN A STRANGE LAND

Copyright © 2011 by Abingdon Press

All rights reserved.

No part of this work may be reproduced or transmitted in any form or by any means, electronic or mechanical, including photocopying and recording, or by any information storage or retrieval system, except as may be expressly permitted by the 1976 Copyright Act or in writing from the publisher. Requests for permission should be addressed to Abingdon Press, P.O. Box 801, 201 Eighth Avenue South, Nashville, TN 37202-0801 or e-mailed to permissions@umpublishing.org.

This book is printed on acid-free paper.

Library of Congress Cataloging-in-Publication Data

Lowery, Joseph (Joseph E.)
Singing the Lord's song in a strange land / Joseph E. Lowery.
   p.   cm.
ISBN 978-1-4267-1324-8 (alk. paper)
   1. Lowery, Joseph (Joseph E.).   2. Civil rights workers—Southern States—Biography. 3. African American civil rights workers—Southern States—Biography.   4. United Methodist Church (U.S.)—Clergy—Biography.   5. Southern Christian Leadership Conference—History. 6. African Americans—Civil rights—Southern States—History—20th century.   7. Civil rights movements—Southern States—History.   8. Selma to Montgomery Rights March (1965 : Selma, Ala.)   9. Southern States—Race relations.   I. Title.
   E185.97.L85A3 2011
   323.092—dc22
   [B]

2010048582

All scripture quotations unless noted otherwise are taken from the King James or Authorized Version of the Bible.

Scripture quotations marked (RSV) are taken from the Revised Standard Version of the Bible, copyright 1952 [2nd edition, 1971] by the Division of Christian Education of the National Council of the Churches of Christ in the United States of America. Used by permission. All rights reserved.

Scripture quotations marked (NIV) are taken from the Holy Bible, NEW INTERNA-TIONAL VERSION®. Copyright © 1973, 1978, 1984 by International Bible Society. All rights reserved throughout the world. Used by permission of International Bible Society.

Scripture quotations marked (ESV) are from The Holy Bible, English Standard Version®, copyright © 2001 by Crossway Bibles, a publishing ministry of Good News Publishers. Used by permission. All rights reserved.

Scripture quotations marked (NLT) are taken from the *Holy Bible*, New Living Translation, copyright © 1996. Used by permission of Tyndale House Publishers, Inc., Wheaton, Illinois 60189. All rights reserved.

11 12 13 14 15 16 17 18 19 20—10 9 8 7 6 5 4 3 2 1

MANUFACTURED IN THE UNITED STATES OF AMERICA

DEDICATION

There are so many, many persons who have meant so much to me and to my career—the thousands who were members of the churches I have served as pastor; the thousands who joined me in marches and demonstrations; the hundreds who called and wrote letters; the millions who prayed for me during my illnesses. I am grateful to all of them—most of whom I don't even know their names.

This effort is dedicated to my wife and children. Without their love and sacrificial assistance, I would have been like a ship at sea, lost in the rain and fog. Because of them, I've been able to "stand the storm."

Evelyn, my wife of over sixty years, has been a good helpmate and lover; she's been a wheel in the middle of a wheel; a shelter, a rudder, and an inspiration. She marched beside me; went to jail; and almost lost her life when Klansmen shot at her car in Decatur, Alabama. She helped our girls grow into beautiful women. She tolerated my foolish ways and cherished my good deeds. She remembered even when I forgot. Thanks, "Ev."

I also must thank the girls—Yvonne, Karen, and Cheryl. Especially Cheryl, who found time to take charge: assembling, researching, editing, and taking on numerous other responsibilities that made *Singing the Lord's Song in a Strange Land* come together. Thanks, girls, and especially you, Cheryl.

CONTENTS

Watch Night Sermons

Farewell, My Sisters

The Forty-fourth President of These United States

The Beat Goes On

FOREWORD

The challenge of Christianity and its followers is how to apply the principles of its Founder in personal living and in the society at large. This inward faith struggle resulted in institutional struggle in the church itself. Theologies sought to address the question of personal piety and social holiness. Eventually, there was even a movement in Protestantism, the Social Gospel Movement, that urged churches and pastors alike to relate the Gospel to the social ills of the day.

For many churches today, the question is still a pressing one. Is the role of the church to save souls or transform social institutions and society itself? Pastors face the same question in their ministry and especially in their preaching. Many avoid social issues in their preaching and in their public witness as well. Others face the issue head-on and respond that the Gospel is both personal and social.

The Reverend Joseph E. Lowery is among those pastors who demonstrate that the message of Jesus Christ is for both the soul and the body; that it is for the individual as well as the community; that it is both personal and public.

But unlike most pastors who merely preach a Social Gospel, Lowery goes a step further by personally engaging himself in the societal issues of social justice and human rights. Lowery is recognized as one of the major leaders of the civil rights movement, where he joined the late Dr. Martin Luther King, Jr., in challenging Jim Crow and segregation, and eventually formed the highly effective Southern Christian Leadership Conference. He put his body and life on the line time and time again. Exposing himself to violence and numerous death threats, he refused to back down from the injustice he saw in his beloved South and throughout the nation.

Yet to identify the Reverend Lowery simply as a civil rights leader, which he was, is to miss his broader leadership as he advocated on behalf of social, political, and economic justice. But one cannot even stop there. In the tradition of Gandhi and King, Lowery was and remains a strong peace advocate. Indeed, leaders across the world call upon him for counsel and advice.

In the pages that follow, one gets a close-up glimpse not just of his philosophy of nonviolent resistance and his courage to speak truth to power, but of his theology, which informs his philosophy and public ministry.

Perhaps the most remarkable aspect of the ministry and career of Dr. Lowery is his commitment to be a local church pastor. The congregation is his first love. Thus, in all his worldwide and public ministry, he remained a United Methodist pastor, serving a local congregation. In part, he proved that a pastor of a congregation could at the same time have a relevant, engaged ministry in the affairs of the public square.

He preached Sunday after Sunday to a congregation. He was a pastor to his flock in times of sadness, struggle, and conflict, and he rejoiced with them in times of celebration. He baptized their children, counseled those who were troubled, and stood with families in times of death. He was a pastor.

The Reverend Joseph Lowery stands in the best prophetic tradition as he challenges unjust systems, inhuman policies, and abusive institutional practices.

The sermons contained in this volume are moving, nurturing, and prophetic. The Reverend Joseph Echols Lowery has demonstrated not only that preaching can be to one's head as well as one's heart, but also that the preached Word can move the hearer as well as the preacher to action on behalf of the dispossessed, marginalized, and oppressed.

Bishop Woodie W. White
Bishop in Residence
Candler School of Theology, Emory University
    and
Chairperson
The Joseph E. Lowery Institute for Justice and Human Rights at Clark Atlanta University
Atlanta, Georgia

INTRODUCTION

This book gives a panoramic view of my life in the movement when I was president of the Southern Christian Leadership Conference and as a pastor-preacher. Throughout my life, I have sought to apply the moral imperatives of my faith to social, economic, and political problems. I never saw a real distinction between the roles. Preaching is designed to help folks make heaven their home *and* to make their homes here heavenly. I believe God moves in mysterious ways—always leading me to be his servant. I see the whole world as God's habitat without dividing life into sacred and secular. All of life is sacred; all life is in God's hands.

Life isn't as orderly as we would like! I heard God's voice calling me to preach his Word in and out of season, in and out of the pulpit! When I'm preaching, I'm not me. I am, as far as I am concerned, God's megaphone.

Life is a strange land, but we are called to preach God's Word in strange circumstances. We must sing the Lord's song, do his will even in and under strange circumstances. Here you will find sermons, speeches, poems, commentaries, and remarks that were made in churches, public forums, rallies, and schools and on the streets. During these several decades, I have preached many of these sermons in different places, so it's hard to be specific about the time and place.

"Singing the Lord's song in a strange land" is how I have tried to exist and serve. It is not just music. It is my witness. It's my truth to power. That's how I'd like to be remembered. I hope I kept the voice of moral force and ethical power to a decibel level that it was heard in the corridors of power.

CHAPTER ONE

IN THE BEGINNING

When the Montgomery Bus Boycott began, I was pastor of the Warren Street Methodist Church in Mobile, Alabama, and serving as president of the Interdenominational Ministerial Alliance. I had met Martin Luther King, Jr., at a seminar in Boston before he was called to Dexter Avenue Baptist Church in Montgomery, and later in Montgomery at a meeting sponsored by the Alabama Council on Human Relations. I made some remarks at the meeting and so did he. Afterwards, we congratulated each other with the usual preacher-to-preacher excesses, and yet with sufficient sincerity that indicated we were genuinely respectful of each other. We promised to stay in touch and even pledged to invite each other to preach in our respective churches. I was his senior by a few years—seven—both in age and in pastoral experience. We developed a friendship that lasted until his tragic death on April 4, 1968. "Through many dangers, toils, and snares..." But I'm getting ahead of myself.

Following the outlawing of the NAACP in Alabama (for refusing to divulge its membership rolls to conniving forces who would surely have found ways to harass them), the Montgomery Improvement Association was organized in Montgomery; the Alabama Christian Movement for Human Rights in Birmingham; and the Alabama Civic Affairs Association in Mobile. Martin headed the Montgomery group; Fred Shuttlesworth, the ACMHR; and I was elected to lead the Mobile organization. In the heat of the movement in the mid-1950s, we would communicate with each other regularly by telephone, and somebody suggested we should meet at least once a month in Montgomery to coordinate, cooperate, and *commiserate*. We usually met on Monday, though not always. We met in Montgomery because it was the center of the state. Ten o'clock in the morning was the designated hour. I would leave Mobile at six o'clock and arrive in the capital at ten. Fred would leave Birmingham at eight and arrive at ten. Martin and Ralph Abernathy would leave their homes in Montgomery at whatever time and arrive at the meeting place at whatever time. Always closer to eleven than ten. We were glad to see one another, and after swapping tales about our great worship services and the great sermons we preached, we would get down to the serious business of the movement. C. G. Gomillion, a professor at Tuskegee and a leader in the movement there, joined us for a spell. I think he got tired of hearing us relive our preaching experiences of the Sunday before, and he dropped out. It was our loss, for he brought great intellectual strength to the table.

These meetings were the genesis of the Southern Christian Leadership Conference. Somebody suggested that we ought to expand the circle and call a meeting of all the folks who were engaged in movements, mostly around bus segregation in the South. The call went out, and we gathered in Atlanta in the fall of 1956. Kelly Miller Smith from Nashville and C. K. Steele from Tallahassee, Florida, were among the preachers who met us at Ebenezer Baptist Church (Daddy King's church) to discuss the feasibility of a South-wide organization to give strength to the movements in local communities and maximize national impact. The meeting was disrupted by the bombing of Ralph's church in Montgomery. Fortunately (no thanks to the perpetrators) no fatalities or injuries were sustained. Undeterred by cowardly acts of terrorism, we met in late January through early February in New Orleans, and SCLC was born, although that name came through a process of semantic evolution. Voter registration as well as transportation were major thrusts and therefore were included in the name, which finally evolved to Southern Christian Leadership Conference. Considerable debate took place over whether the inclusion of *Christian* meant exclusion of members of other faiths. We concluded that members of any faith could belong so long as they embraced the principles of the fatherhood of God, the brotherhood of man, and the efficacy of nonviolence in a movement for achieving social change.

The Montgomery bus boycott was the center and core of the newborn civil rights movement, which brought new dimensions to the struggle for liberation and first-class citizenship. The most significant among these, in my opinion, was the element of *self-determination*. When more than fifty thousand Black folks decided that the *back of the bus* was no longer tolerable and that, no matter what anybody said, they were not going to ride in the back of the bus, that was a child born in the crib of the old Confederacy and rocked into the cradle of an emerging democracy. It did not matter what the courts said, or what the city council said, or what legislative bodies did or did not enact: *we were finished with the back of the bus!*

Martin's leadership in the boycott, which brought him into international prominence even then, made him the natural choice for the first president of the newly formed rights group SCLC. Not even the most cynical could dispute the indisputable: the call to the pulpit of Dexter Avenue Baptist Church was divine intervention. It was a perfect union: Martin by training and temperament; Montgomery by geographics and demographics; and the buses by the universality of usage and the commonality of abuses. (Other cities experienced "back of the bus policies," including Mobile, where I pastored. Mobile was as racist as Montgomery, but its racism was not as toxic as Montgomery's and Birmingham's.) The bus (public transit) was the common denominator in the community. Nobody needed to persuade the people that Rosa Parks's refusal to give up her seat to a white passenger represented the feelings of all "colored" patrons, for everyone who ever rode the bus had felt the sting of abuse and denigration. They were all tired of having to stand up so whites could sit down. Even Black folks who didn't ride the bus had a mama or an auntie or a brother or a papa who did and who had drunk from the bitter cup of humiliation they all shared in this common denominator, this racial discriminator, this dehumanizer. So, experientially and vicariously, all fifty thousand took the boycott personally and seriously! It was the most effective mass movement in our history! There were earlier boycotts, but none lasted as long or worked so well. In addition to the common denominator factor, the movement had the inspired leadership of Martin Luther King, Jr., who brought, in eloquent fashion, the moral imperatives of our faith to bear on the critical areas of racial oppression. We were no longer content to just preach about making heaven our home, but felt called to make our homes here heavenly. That certainly included living with dignity and resisting the dehumanizing policies and practices that drove us to the back of the bus, the front of the train, the balcony of theaters, the end of the line, the basement of opportunities.

The elements of faith and self-determination were new factors that brought strength and excitement to the movement. Later, Black students would catch the spirit of self-determination and take destiny into their hands. They would reject the inconsistency of being able to buy safety pins at any counter while being restricted to buying a sandwich from the "colored" counter, if any. The students were roughed up, to put it mildly, at some places and beaten viciously at others. No matter, they had "made up minds," and the back of the bus and segregated lunch counters in five-and-dime stores were history. It would take the courts much longer to make up their minds, but Black folks in Montgomery and in North Carolina and across the South rendered the only verdicts that mattered—no more segregation, no more back of the bus!

While the courts did eventually issue clear decisions on segregation in public transportation, I'm not sure we ever really learned what the courts would say clearly about the sit-ins. The 1964 Public Accommodations Act came much later, and the matter passed into history. That is not to say that everyone everywhere had heard about desegregation in public places as late as the last of the 1970s and early 1980s. I visited sugar plantations in Louisiana during the Carter administration seeking to find a handle for helping workers escape the torture of life on those plantations, and I ran into an eating place near Lafayette that had a "colored" entrance in the rear of the premises! A strange land!

A strange land requires a familiar song. That's why members of the community of faith sing the Lord's song in this strange land.

So the Southern Christian Leadership Conference was born in New Orleans in early 1957. The philosophy of nonviolence was translated and transposed into techniques and strategies for opposing segregation and discrimination based on race and color. Nonviolent direct action is more than passive resistance; it is dynamic insistence; it is sometimes civil disobedience to man's unjust laws; but it is also spiritual obedience to the laws of a higher power. It is refusing to get up so that a white person can sit down; it is also joining white people on the voting rolls so we both can enjoy the fruits of representative government. It is not only changing the color of government; it is seeking to change the character of government as well. The struggle against segregation in public accommodations exploded in Birmingham, where Fred Shuttlesworth provided courageous leadership that laid the groundwork for the massive movement that followed his invitation to Martin to bring the Southern Christian Leadership Conference to Birmingham. The Alabama Christian Movement for Human Rights (ACMHR) headed by Shuttlesworth saw the need for a national movement ushered in by SCLC and Martin. New dimensions of nonviolent direct action blossomed in Birmingham, which was known as the "Johannesburg of the South." While Montgomery introduced the element of massive withdrawal, Birmingham initiated the mighty force of mass jail-ins. Never in our history had we challenged the fearful hammer of imprisonment held over our heads. It was an intimidating and cruel factor in southern life. In most southern communities, law enforcement was lily white at every level. Prison was dreaded by Black folks and for good reason. All manner of abuse, sometimes fatal, went unchallenged behind prison walls, where only the eyes of white officials could gaze, and the word of a Black prisoner (when one dared speak) meant little or nothing against that of white officials. But in Birmingham the sting was removed or at least softened for a while. There weren't enough jails to hold the throngs of adults and then, thank God, youths who marched as sainted pilgrims into the cells, which (like Paul's and Silas's) were transformed into prayer cells and sanctuaries. The back of segregation in public accommodations was broken.

I sat in Governor Clement's office in Nashville when he called the president of Morrison's Cafeterias in Mobile, Alabama, and urged him to desegregate his cafeterias in Nashville, where sit-ins were shattering the "peace" of the city. The president of Morrison's (now Piccadilly) turned the governor down and told him that he would never see his restaurants serve Blacks in non-segregated fashion. If memory serves me correctly, the Public Accommodations Act took effect in the summer of 1964, and Morrison's, along with other restaurants in the South, were desegregated. The president of Morrison's passed away shortly thereafter. He kept his word!

No right of citizenship is more sacred than the right to vote. And so, board and staff met with Martin in Birmingham in 1964 to strategize for a campaign to gain the right to vote. Selma, Alabama, was chosen as the base community. It was in the Black Belt of Alabama, which had a majority Black population but had no Black elected officials and had only a handful of Black citizens registered to vote. The Student Nonviolent Coordinating Committee had begun a campaign, but the racist courts had forbidden them to even assemble peacefully. We decided to strengthen their efforts. The rest is colorful history. The ugliness of racist oppression was personified in Sheriff Jim Clark. The beauty of a struggle for right and righteousness was personified in the demonstrators at the courthouse, on the bridge, in the streets and jails.

Montgomery gave birth to massive withdrawal; Birmingham, to massive jailings. Marion and Selma were the birthplaces of the pilgrimage from Selma to Montgomery for the right to vote. Hosea Williams and John Lewis led the Bloody Sunday march. Martin led the pilgrimage those historic fifty miles to the steps of the capitol, where he asked the eternal interrogative: *How long?* And answered: *Not long!* At the close of that speech in March 1965, Martin named a committee to take the demands of the march to the governor. Governor Wallace said he would meet only with Alabama residents. I was pastoring in Birmingham so he named me to chair the committee, which included businessman A. G. Gaston, lawyers Orzell Billingsley and Fred Gray, and University of Tuskegee president Dr. Luther Foster, among others. The National Guard had been federalized, and a general was in charge. I asked if we had been cleared to climb the steps to the door of the capitol to take the document to Governor Wallace. The general made a phone call, and I assumed his nod meant we had been cleared. But when we started up the steps, the blue sea (state patrol officers) blocked our progress. I looked at the general, and he barked some military commands, and uniformed members of the national guard stationed themselves in front of the troopers and placed their bayonets across their chests and barked some military sounds. The blue sea parted—and we walked through on dry land up the capitol steps. There, the governor's secretary said he would take the petition. I refused. We hadn't walked fifty miles to give the demands to the governor's secretary. We walked away. A few days later the secretary called and said the governor had decided to meet with a few members of the committee, the chair not included! *All or no one at all,* the committee retorted. A few days later the entire committee met with the governor for ninety minutes.

And then there were two! Two monumental pieces of legislation: the 1964 Public Accommodations Act and the 1965 Voting Rights Act. One wiped away the stain of legalized segregation in public places, while the other opened a new world of political emancipation. When Martin died in 1968, there were only a few hundred Black elected officials; today the number approaches ten thousand. Black voters have made the difference in critical elections nationally as well as in state and local governments. The face of government has changed forever!

On April 4, 1968, the hate-monster of domestic terrorism fired a shot in Memphis that echoed around the world. Martin Luther King, Jr., was killed. We may never know exactly *who* did it, but we know *what* did it. One year earlier in New York's Riverside Church, Martin described the triple-headed monster that plagued civilization: militarism, materialism (greed), and racism. Martin's death ignited fires of varied stripes across the nation. They killed the dreamer and put a severe hurting on the dream. The dream survived; the hurt remains. Martin's indelible stamp on SCLC rendered Ralph Abernathy's job difficult to say the least. To many, the movement died with Martin. Christianity did not perish with Christ's crucifixion. Nor did the movement die with Martin. It was crippled, yes, but God moves, still. We will always miss his eloquent voice, but the presence of his message and his mission continues to motivate and inspire.

Ralph fought a good fight, but no one could fill Martin's shoes. Ralph said he tried. While understandable, it was probably not the wisest course. Media were skeptical, even hostile. Civil rights occupied a place on the media priority scale two notches below the snail darter. Ralph was an able preacher, an excellent pastor, and a good president, and he kept the ship afloat through the Poor People's Campaign and Resurrection City. He helped put the issues surrounding poverty on the national agenda. It became increasingly difficult to raise adequate funding to expand programs for an agenda that expanded with or without funding. Neither President Nixon nor his cabinet was sympathetic to the movement. Executive staff in SCLC, loyal to Martin, now sought other corridors through which to move their energies. Ralph waged a valiant effort but grew weary of having to fight on many fronts with fewer troops. So he too sought other corridors and offered himself as a candidate for Congress. He became the beloved president emeritus of SCLC until his death.

The chairman of the board (JEL) was given the position of acting president (while retaining the board chairmanship), and a search committee started looking in February for a president to be elected in August 1977. The state of Georgia, meanwhile, provided the first president from the Deep South in modern history—Jimmy Carter—and the acting president and board of SCLC jump-started the year by holding the first Black organization meeting with the new president of these United States. I never planned to be president of SCLC. Vice president and chairman of the board—supporting the president and encouraging the board to be more supportive—were all I sought. Between February and August 1977, the board and convention decided otherwise, and at Ebenezer Church in August 1977, I became the third president of the Southern Christian Leadership Conference.

***

Intensifying our involvement in foreign affairs, extending the economic empowerment phase of programmatic thrust, deepening the activism in voter registration and education, stopping the violence, initiating down-with-dope programs, and seeking to provide good housing for low- and moderate-income families were among the major programs and policies of the twenty-one Lowery years. The lack of interest of the press, the difficulty in raising funds, and the rising costs of operations continued to plague the organization; but through it all, God remained faithful as we remained faithful to the legacies of King and Abernathy. We participated in extending the Voting Rights Act upon its expiration in 1970, 1975, and particularly in 1982; and called and settled a boycott of Winn-Dixie Supermarkets following the finding that the Southeast U.S. chain had knowingly relabeled canned pears, peaches, and fish to cover their South African origins.

The story continues...

CHAPTER TWO

I REMEMBER MARTIN

1980

I *remember Martin...*

whose eloquent voice sounded and resounded the cries of freedom on behalf of the poor and oppressed.

I remember Martin...

for the warmth of his person, which made even me feel comfortable in the presence of his greatness, and for the challenge that I felt to do more and more because he did so much and became so much.

I remember Martin...

for his ability to attract the support of such diverse personalities as those of us who made up the board and staff and how he inspired us to forge those differences into united forces against the common enemies of hatred and bias—yet without destroying the diversities that made us creative and effective most of the time to move mountains.

I remember Martin...

who, more than any other human being in our time, touched the conscience of a mighty and rich nation so that it was moved to institute the social change that lifted burdens from the weak and gave new dignity to the poor.

I remember Martin...

because his dream was in essence the dream of a nation that had forgotten—and more than that, it was in truth the dream of a Creator who had not forgotten and who made "of one blood all nations of men to dwell upon the face of His earth."

I remember Martin...

as a conditioning force in challenging the conscience of the nation and the world to bring "justice...down as waters, and righteousness as a mighty stream."

In his spirit, SCLC—his organization, his heart, his ministry—with God's help shall continue to fulfill the dream in the streets and in the suites. They have killed the dreamer; we must make sure they cannot kill the dream.

The dream must be translated into sustained effort to bring about the systematic change needed to commit the nation to full employment; to put an end to repressive criminal justice systems; to bring peace with justice to all the world; to usher in the day of brotherhood and end the long night of wrong.

yes, I remember Martin...

as the fullest embodiment of the calling to ministry—and I am humbled and frightened and challenged to occupy the chair where he sat as president of this organization, SCLC. And yet I know that I have his love, and in those lonely hours I sense his presence and—more than that—we walk with God, whose will is surely liberty for all his children—and he has promised that we shall overcome.

CHAPTER THREE

THE DEATH PENALTY: A MATTER OF PLACE AND RACE, INEQUITY AND INIQUITY

Ebenezer Baptist Church, Atlanta, Georgia, Early 1990s

The death penalty is a matter of place and race and inequity and iniquity. The place is definitely in the southern states of the United States. More than one-half of the persons on death row are in the South, and 92 percent of the executions in 1972 were right here in our own state of Georgia. Georgia is among the bottom five states in education and among the top four in executions. Since 1973, Georgia has executed fourteen people. The death penalty is a matter of place.

The prosecuting attorneys used 80 to 90 percent of their jury strikes to remove African American citizens who were serving on jury rolls. The death penalty is a matter of place.

In the early years of the country, the state constitutions in most of the southern states set forth the race of the victim in a capital crime as the prime factor, moreso than the nature of the crime itself. The death penalty is a matter of place.

> THE SUPREME COURT'S DECISION IN *MCCLESKEY V. KEMP* ACTS AS A SUBSTANTIAL BARRIER TO THE ELIMINATION OF RACIAL INEQUALITIES IN THE CRIMINAL JUSTICE SYSTEM, PERPETUATING AN UNFAIR RACIAL IMBALANCE THAT HAS COME TO DEFINE CRIMINAL JUSTICE IN AMERICA.

The district attorneys are the officers who decide for the most part whether the death penalty will be sought. As in most of the South, nearly all the district attorneys in Georgia are white. The death penalty is a matter of place.

Senator Ted Kennedy offered an amendment to the drug legislation that called for the death penalty for certain drug pushers. The amendment was not to abolish or eliminate the death penalty but simply to suggest and require that it not be administered with racial bias. All the senators of this place, the South, voted against that amendment except one, Senator James Ralph Sassor. The death penalty is a matter of place.

In one Alabama county, the prosecutor in his notes rated prospective jurors: A—strong, B—medium, C—weak, D—Black. The death penalty is a matter of place.

In the southern states the death penalty is an attraction, and it is a fatal attraction. It is a matter of place in Georgia. Georgia's Ocmulgee judicial circuit is made up of seven counties containing districts that are almost half Black. In 22 capital cases involving Black defendants, the district attorney down there, Joe Wiley, competes with another district attorney in North Carolina for the title of the "Killing DA." He used 169 of his jury strikes against Blacks and only 19 against whites. The death penalty is a matter of place.

There have been 28 capital cases tried in the Ocmulgee circuit since 1973, and 22 of those involved Black defendants. That district has only one-third the population of Fulton County, Georgia [Atlanta]. The death penalty is a matter of place.

In Greene County, Georgia, one-half the population is Black, yet two Black males were sentenced to death in Greene County, and in each case there were only whites on the jury. Georgia has 137 Superior Court judges, and only 5 are Black. The death penalty is largely a matter of place.

Of the 103 executions that occurred in 1976, 60 percent took place in Texas, Florida, Louisiana, and Georgia. Ninety percent of all executions occurred in the South. The death penalty is a matter of place.

We have already mentioned, in terms of *place,* how Blacks as prosecutors, judges, and jurors are excluded from the process, all the way from arrest to execution. All those persons overwhelmingly are white. The death penalty is a matter of race. Since 1976, no whites have been executed for killing a Black. The death penalty is a matter of race.

In Florida, for the killing of whites, you are 37 times more likely to get the death penalty than for the killing of Blacks. In Georgia you are 10 times more likely, and in Maryland 6 times more likely. In other words, Black life is viewed as cheaper than white life. The death penalty is a matter of race.

The death penalty is a matter of inequity. Poor people cannot afford quality legal counsel. Poor people make up almost 100 percent of those sentenced to death. The death penalty is imposed on those who are poor and disadvantaged. Most persons on death row are unemployed or employed at minimum-wage level at the time of their arrest. The death penalty is a matter of inequity.

In 1973, Supreme Court Justice William O. Douglas observed "that one can search in vain for the execution of any member of the affluent in our society." The poor are more likely to be represented by court-appointed lawyers. The death penalty is a matter of inequity.

I think sin is involved in the death penalty. It is crystal clear that no human being has the right to take another human being's life. This is the principle of capital punishment—seeks to defend. But it's really the principle that capital punishment corrupts. The time has come for us to renounce violence.

As a means of resolving situations, violence never will; it indulges the desire for revenge without seeking to redress the underlying causes of crime, poverty, illiteracy, mental illness, despair, desperation. It is iniquity because it violates the sacredness of human life, given to us as a lease from God. It is iniquity because the Supreme Court in the McCleskey case reached back and claimed the Dred Scott procedure, when the court acknowledged the inherent wrong in the death penalty but would not address the wrong. The death penalty is a matter of inequity and iniquity.

By embracing the executioner, we invest in a morally bankrupt symbol and an ineffective, unjust solution of social conflict. The death penalty is a matter of place and race. The death penalty is a matter of inequity and iniquity.

So let us resolve in all our hearts and minds to let go of the decade of the 1980s; except for the fact that I'm a decade older, I'm glad to see those years go. It was a decade of decadence, a decade of descent, a decade of denial, a decade of degeneration. We must make the decade of the 1990s a decade of "Do the right thing," a decade of redemption, a decade of regeneration, a decade of revitalization.

You and I, in the coalition of conscience, must make it right. If we don't do it, who will? If we don't do it now, it will be too late. We must make the death penalty a thing of the past. If South Africa is turning its face toward dismantling apartheid and can declare a moratorium on the death penalty, we ought to hear clearly the message God is speaking. So I say, if this is to be a decade for "Do the right thing," it must be the decade of the coalition of conscience, the decade of activism; we must get up off our complacency.

We must escape from our defeatism. We can make a difference; we can turn the tide.

****

Let me tell you, in 1964, after we passed the Civil Rights Act, Martin took some of us to see Lyndon Johnson to tell him we couldn't vote. He said, "Tell the boys we just passed the Civil Rights Act. . . . We can't pass another one."

"But, Mr. President, we can't vote."

"I understand that, but we can't have another Civil Rights Act. We just passed the Public Accommodations Act."

We went back to Birmingham and rented room 30 in the A. G. Gaston Hotel. We stayed there day and night and strategized and planned the Selma movement, and we went to Selma and marched and prayed. We were beaten and slain, but we kept on marching and organizing and agitating and conjugating and incarcerating. But after a while regeneration came in, and people from all over the country came to Selma/Montgomery, and we went back to Mr. Johnson. We said, "Mr. Johnson, you said you couldn't pass another Civil Rights Act. Here, we wrote one for you; sign it." You remember, he went on national TV, signed it, and said, "We shall overcome."

15

I'm saying today that as the coalition of conscience in the decade of the 1990s, we must go back to Starkville, to Atlanta—wherever we must go—to Jackson, to Gulfport. Wherever we must go! But this must be a decade of activism until the right legislation wipes out the death penalty and makes the decade of the 1990s a decade of "Do the right thing."

CHAPTER FOUR

ECONOMIC POWER
OF THE VOTE: ADDRESS AT
THE SOUTHERN CHRISTIAN
LEADERSHIP CONFERENCE
ANNUAL CONVENTION

New Orleans, Louisiana, July 30, 1995

It's fitting that we hold this thirty-eighth convention in New Orleans. It is here that we initiated this journey. It is here now that we must chart a new strategy, a new movement. Since we last met in Dallas last year, there's a new kid on the block. He's a bully, a mean-spirited bully who is on the block, carrying a big stick, talking loud, talking trash, and meaning the country and us no good. Most bullies don't mean anyone any good, but like most bullies, they are more sound than substance. They are more of a symbol than one with sense. You simply have to understand that when you stand up to fight and you mean business, usually bullies will take flight. We must prepare a strategy.

New Orleans has a fascinating history. You can't come here without talking about this land of Basin Street. There's jazz and Louis, gospel and Mahalia, Mardi Gras, the Superdome, gumbo, its third black mayor, sensitive statesmen, and the birthplace of the man who introduced me today. He's a reverend, congressman, and ambassador—Andrew Young. New Orleans is the city where the mightiest of our rivers meets the sea. In Ecclesiastes it says all rivers run into the sea. The Mississippi begins as a little stream up in faraway Minnesota, but it looks southward to begin its historic journey. It glances affectionately at Iowa, winks at Wisconsin, kisses Illinois on the cheek, but moves on to Missouri. It tarries in

17

St. Louis long enough for W. C. Handy to stand on one shore and look on the other and say, "I got a lover on the other side." It invented the blues, saying, "Mississippi River running deep and wide, you know you got my baby on the other side." But the river couldn't stay there and nurture its broken heart. It had to roll on toward Memphis while workers sang, "Tote that barge, lift that bale." The river went on to Memphis, and there it embraced Beale Street and said hello and good-bye at the same time. But the river had to roll on. It had a date with the Delta in Mississippi where it softened the soil and enriched the magnolias. Meanwhile, the old river became a watery grave to victims of racist hate and deadly violence. But it kept on rolling. It bends in New Orleans, but it doesn't break. And at last, it reaches the welcoming arms of the sea.

We left New Orleans in 1957 with a new technique called non-violence. It was new in the context of American struggle, but as old as Gandhi, as experienced as Thoreau, and as ancient as a young Galilean. And with the spirit of the river flowing toward the sea to be free, that movement made its way to South Africa and to the Philippines, and from Selma to Soweto. The spirit of that battle from New Orleans challenged the morality of war and moved across the world to introduce a new era of social justice and sensitivity to the need for human dignity. So we come here in 1995 like the river with a new journey but an old mission. We come to talk about focusing on the essentials—political, economic, and spiritual empowerment.

On the thirtieth anniversary of that march that gave us our voting rights, we march to remind us not only of the pain and the suffering that gave birth to the Voting Rights Act, but also of the pain that comes when we don't use that right won thirty years ago from Selma to Montgomery. Twenty-five thousand votes or less would have made a difference in the election last November. Those twenty-five thousand votes or less could have been cast by us, and they would have changed who would have been Speaker of the House. But we have to understand that the political process is not something you play seesaw with; you don't enter into it when you feel like it and give it up when you don't. The political process is that which determines public policy, and that which determines public policy is that which has a lot to do with the quality of life. We're all God's children, and if you're God's child, you cannot afford to neglect or ignore or be careless about public policy. We can never again let a minority of voters put in power people who are in a mood of malice and who are willing to turn back the clock because we are willing to sit down on our rusty dusties and not get up and exercise the right we won thirty years ago in Selma.

Yes, public policy is important. There is a Supreme Court that has five confused people—three white males, one white female, and a whatchamacallhim. The whatchamacallhim is the most confused of them all. Whatchamacallhim is from Pinpoint, Georgia, and I just don't understand his thinking. Members of SCLC met with him for two hours and said, "The people in Georgia want us to give you the benefit of the doubt. They want to think that you've been playing these games because you looked at the highway to glory and you saw the Democratic lane was crowded. Then you looked over into the Republican lane and saw it wasn't crowded at all. So you decided to take the least traveled highway, and you made it on up to the top. But we figured that you were just playing a game and that when you got there and you were free as you could be—nobody is freer than a Supreme Court justice— you'd come to your senses and you would stop playing games." And he said to us: "I know what Martin Luther King stood for, and I know what you stand for. If I make it to the Court, you will not be ashamed of me." Well, I wrote him a letter the other day. I said, "Whatchamacallhim, I'm ashamed of you." It is tragic that the swing vote—the pivotal, critical, decisive vote on the Supreme Court—rests in the hands of a 1995 whatchamacallhim. But we can't stop there. The river has to flow on to its destiny, into the sea of justice and the sea of liberation. We can't stop there and keep worrying about him. We have to exercise that which determines public policy. It doesn't make any difference what whatchamacallhim does. If we vote right and vote consistently, we will put in office and keep in office a president whose next appointment to the Supreme Court will not be a whatchamacallhim. That's public policy at work. You get on the Supreme Court by an appointment by the president. The president is elected by voters. So if you're mad about Clarence Thomas, vote! When you say, "It doesn't make any difference whether I vote or not," think about whatchmacallhim.

Therefore, like the river, we must keep on rolling. There's nothing more important on our agenda today—if we deal with the essentials of political empowerment—than voter registration, voter education, and voter participation. Don't let anybody fool you. It is important. It is significant. It is essential. And if you do not vote, you are not a good Christian. I am serious about that. I think folks who don't vote are flirting with hell. Because what you are doing is not using that which people fought, bled, and died for and what God gave us. God moved in a mysterious way. God moved us from Selma to Montgomery. God sent Viola Liuzzo, a white woman, to show it wasn't just a Black issue. Voting is a sacred human issue transcending race and gender. You and I have to raise the level of morality in the context of public policy and voting. We must see to it that we don't have a heartless legislative branch, and we don't need a fainthearted executive branch. We have to send a message to the administration. When I met with President Clinton a week ago Friday, before he delivered his affirmative action speech, I said quite frankly to him: "With a heartless Congress, we don't need a fainthearted executive. Stand up and be counted! If you lose, lose on principle. If you lose, lose doing the right thing."

I used to play softball. I tried to play baseball, but the ball was too hard for me. What I hated was to be called out on strikes with the bat on my shoulder. I mean, that just hurt me. It hurts me now to see a good batter stand up there, and the man says, "Three strikes, you're out!" and he hasn't even taken a swing at it. Even if you miss it, swing at it because you will never know what you could hit until you do. I guarantee that you will never get any hits if you don't take a swing at the ball.

When I met my wife, she was a preacher's daughter. I took her out for the first time. When we got home, on the porch, I didn't know whether to ask her to kiss me good night or not. This was the first time I'd been out with a preacher's daughter, so I wasn't sure. I turned and started down the steps. Then I stopped and said, "Shoot, I'm gonna swing at it." I got a hit too!

I was proud of Brother Clinton when he stood up to make his remarks on affirmative action. I was proud that he swung at it, and I think he got a hit. We must have courageous, bold politicians and those who mold public policy. But we wrestle here with a serious issue. We must wrestle with maximizing the impact of our vote. You see, the thing about voting rights and Black politicians, we did not bleed and die to get the Voting Rights Act to change just the color of government but to change the character of government. And so it's important that they hear from us. It's an issue of conscience, an issue of morality. We must learn to have impact in districts where we are a minority and help the nation understand, in spite of what the Court said, what diverse interaction means. The most interactive, in terms of crossing racial lines in districts, are those districts that are majority Black. The most interactive district that I know of in Georgia is District 11 where Cynthia McKinney is the congresswoman and they have just a few more Blacks than they do whites. There's real interaction. She goes out of her way to make sure the white folks understand that she represents their interests, too. Sanford Bishop's district is the same way. So when the courts talk about diversity, it is not resegregation to have a majority minority district. It is the essence of diversity. And the trouble with white folks is that they don't want to recognize the diversity of districts where Black folks hold the balance of power and where there is Black leadership. White folks can't understand. They'll let you integrate the neighborhood until they think you're going to become the majority. Then they're like the three blind mice. See how they run.

A reporter with the Atlanta *Constitution* once said to me that the church is the most segregated institution, and then he asked why. I told him this was something I'd studied, and I proceeded to explain. It's not that white folks don't like to hear Black folks preach. They love to hear Black folks preach. When Andy Young was running for governor, he told me he thought he was going to be elected because when he went down to a south Georgia town, white folks turned out to hear him. I told him they weren't coming to vote for him; they were coming to hear him preach. They love to hear us sing. They will walk a mile—not for a Camel—but to hear Black folks sing. But the reason they don't join Black churches is that the head knocker in the church is a Black person, and they can't deal with Black leadership. But if they're going to heaven, they may find a surprise. I've checked it out. I had a good look at God, and she's black!

While we seek political power to deal with public policy, Black people must organize at every level. There is no room for apathy. And I really don't think it's apathy; it's more disillusionment. Our expectations were too high. We thought that once we had a Black elected official, all our problems would go away. We thought that when we sent Andy to Congress from the fifth district in Atlanta, every Black man was going to get instantly healthy, wealthy, and wise. We were just as poor when he came out as when he went in. But there were many other things that were improved. And you can't expect Black officials to undo in thirty years what it took white folks three hundred years to mess up. So we had to understand that our expectations were too high. We had to bring them down to reality and understand that no matter what the situation is, we cannot afford to neglect the political process.

Regarding the issue of economic empowerment—we must work diligently. I cannot emphasize this too much. We've got to stop going around blaming other folks for our problems. I was in Panama City, Florida, yesterday attending a funeral. The police there shot a nineteen-year-old Black lad twice in the back and killed him. I went there because I was asked to come and give his eulogy. I was also asked to organize a march, and there were eight hundred people who participated. We marched across Panama City, but I told them the next time we march, we'll do it on those sandy white beaches that are in all the advertisements. They are beautiful. But if you mess with those beaches, you'll get everyone's attention. That's where the money is. There's something wrong with a city that cares more for its beaches than its babies. Those police officers felt comfortable killing that Black lad because we, Black people, have been sent a message that Black life is cheap and that we think it's cheap too. Black males have killed more young Black males in ten years than the Ku Klux

Klan killed in more than one hundred years. We've sent that message, and the blame is on us. The river is on us. We must make up our minds that if there's going to be a new movement, we must initiate it. If there's going to be change, we have to implement it. Nobody else is going to do it for us.

We have to demand equitable reinvestment from the private sector. That's a strategy we must embrace right now. Look around when you spend your money and see who works there. See what the management situation is. Find out if they engage in equitable reinvestment in our communities. We've got to stop spending our money where the money never comes back into our community. We have to teach our dollars some sen$e by investing and pooling our resources and supporting Black-owned businesses. We also have to support those other-owned businesses that support us.

Operation Breadbasket is alive. We've signed two covenants this year that amount to about $250 million over the next four or five years. That's money that will be coming back into Black communities. One is with Publix supermarkets, and the other is with Shoney's. Thank God for what's happening in the Olympics.

We were determined to put Blacks in positions to advance economic participation. How embarrassing it would be to have the Olympics in Atlanta and not have Blacks participating at every level. No economic enterprise can be sacrificed. We are fighting for our lives!

Since I'm in New Orleans, let's talk about the Sugar Bowl. In the early years of the Southern Christian Leadership Conference (SCLC), it was this group that made the Sugar Bowl integrate its executive

OPERATION BREADBASKET (1962–1972) WAS FORMED BY THE SCLC IN ATLANTA IN RESPONSE TO THE POOR TREATMENT BLACKS RECEIVED IN RETAIL STORES AND POOR HIRING AND JOB ADVANCEMENT PRACTICES. THE GROUP ORGANIZED SUCCESSFUL BOYCOTTS AND NEGOTIATED WITH COMPANIES TO HIRE BLACK WORKERS, BRINGING MILLIONS OF DOLLARS INTO BLACK COMMUNITIES.

decision-making staff. But now the organizers of the football tournament have slid back. We need an alive, viable, vibrant, meaningful SCLC movement in New Orleans, and New Orleans needs to respond to the movement! We cannot afford to ignore this deed in the city where the SCLC was born. The Sugar Bowl needs to be checked out. Who sits on the executive committee? Who makes the decisions? How many Black businesses benefit from the Sugar Bowl? Stop worrying about who wins the game. It doesn't matter a cotton-picking nickel who wins the game. What matters is who participates in the economic enterprises of the Sugar Bowl. Who counts money when the Sugar Bowl is over? Check it out. Every major economic enterprise must come under our scrutiny if we are to empower ourselves economically.

Now here is an example of Black folk exercising economic power. The Urban League voted not to hold its convention in California next year because of the governor's anti-affirmative action policies. Every group meeting in California needs to cancel going there. We have to fight back! We have to say in every instance that attempts to strangle us: we'll fight back! We have to help America understand that affirmative action is not just good for minorities and women. Affirmative action is good business for all Americans. It's good business to practice diversity and justice. It's good business to be inclusive. We have to help America understand she is better off because she has enjoyed the contributions of the diversity of her population.

I remember a story Dr. Harry V. Richardson told me when he was chaplain at Tuskegee Institute. He was traveling by train from Tuskegee to Birmingham, and he was in the section of the building where Blacks waited at the train station. The colored waiting room didn't have a good roof, and it was pouring down rain. Harry was getting wet, and there was a white man standing in the section for white travelers. Harry could tell the white man was uneasy watching him get soaked. But Harry didn't go into the covered area because he didn't want any trouble. After a while, the white man finally said, "Harry, come inside. It's not good for me for you to be out there."

It's not good for America to exclude any of her people. And the two key words in affirmative action are *inclusiveness* and *justice*. It is not reverse discrimination. It is not preferential treatment. It is including those who have been traditionally excluded. Jesus practiced affirmative action. Jesus taught affirmative action. He said that those who are well don't need a physician, but those who are sick do. Here's something else. A man had two sons. One went out into the world, and one was home comfortable and well taken care of. The father told the son at home that he was all right and that he was loved. The father didn't mean to neglect that son, but he needed to go out and see about the boy who was lost. Every evening before the father went to bed, he looked down the side of the property to see if his son was coming home. That's affirmative action! I heard Jesus when he talked about a woman who had ten coins and lost one of them. Nine of the coins were safe, but she tore up the house until she found the coin that was lost. That's affirmative action. I also heard Jesus say there was a man with one hundred sheep, and ninety-nine were tucked away comfortably. The ninety-nine had ranch houses with three-car garages; ninety-nine had a television in every room; ninety-nine had health care and adequate insurance; and ninety-nine had incomes in the top brackets. But one little sheep—it must have been a little black sheep—was out in the wilderness with no health insurance, no Medicare, no Medicaid, no housing, no opportunities. The shepherd didn't neglect the ninety-nine, but he said he had to go out and find the one lost sheep. That's affirmative action.

Darkness is all around us. It's stormy and cloudy outside, but I think we ought to march. The people of New Orleans need to see that we care. I think it sends a message. Don't let anybody fool you about marching. A lot of Negroes say it's out of style. Well, what is your suggestion? Marching is significant. It gets the attention of the community. It makes people aware that there are some lost sheep out there and we ought to go get them. Joshua marched. And when he marched, all of heaven responded. That marching brought the walls of Jericho down, and we need to march to bring down some walls. If you don't march, don't hinder me.

CHAPTER FIVE

UNDERSTANDING OUR SILVER RIGHTS: REFLECTIONS

My father always wanted to be a businessman. He also wanted to be a pharmacist. A man sold him two pool tables, and he opened a little amusement parlor. He decided to run the business for a few years and save some money and go to Meharry Medical College in Nashville for pharmacy school. That was the plan, but his business expanded to include a sweet shop, and he ended up running his businesses in Huntsville for about sixty years. My father never went back to his original desire to become a pharmacist.

He adjusted from this setback, and he began to work in the community and the church. My mother was always very active, and he was always supportive of her. He became more active in church after I grew up, later assuming the role of treasurer at Lakeside Methodist Episcopal. This seemed to coincide with my going into the ministry. The church is still in Huntsville, although its location has changed. I used to wonder how my father's life—and my life—would have changed had he been able to go after his dream to become a pharmacist. So many Blacks had to abandon

OPERATION HOPE IS A NON-PROFIT ORGANIZATION THAT WAS FOUNDED IMMEDIATELY AFTER THE CIVIL UNREST IN LOS ANGELES, CALIFORNIA, AFTER A JURY ACQUITTED FOUR POLICE OFFICERS IN THE RODNEY KING TRIAL. THE ORGANIZATION PROVIDES ECONOMIC DEVELOPMENT TRAINING, FINANCIAL LITERACY, AND INVESTMENT INITIATIVES TO MARGINALIZED COMMUNITIES.

their dreams while facing the realities of racism and economic limitations. Things have certainly changed from those times, but there are still economic disparities that stand in the way of Black people achieving parity.

SPEECH AT THE OPERATION HOPE CONFERENCE
Atlanta, Georgia, April 12, 2005

The disparities between the haves and the have-nots in this country are a disgraceful, shameful factor of life, second only to the war in Iraq in a betrayal of the American dream. I read a study that somebody did in Sweden. It centered on what would be the fair differential between the average salary of a worker in a plant and the average income of a CEO. The result of that study was that the CEO ought to earn on an average five to seven times more than the average worker. Now, does anybody want to guess what it is in this country? Over 200 times. I suggest that that is an intolerable condition. And those who are courageous enough to try to democratize something called capitalism have their work cut out for them.

During the movement, we used to talk about "silver rights." The Poor People's Campaign was an outgrowth of our desire for this, and Operation Breadbasket was the arm of the SCLC that dealt with silver rights—or economic justice. We didn't invent the idea. We borrowed it from Leon Sullivan, who had a program in Philadelphia, and we embellished it. All the preachers in the SCLC got together and looked at the corporate community and tried to discern what was fair and what ought to flow from the profit-laden coffers of the corporate community into the consumer-deprived coffers of the community.

One of the first battles we had in Atlanta was with Coca-Cola. One of the objectives of the Poor People's Campaign was to get the private sector to commit itself to economic justice. Not charity, but parity. I remember our group arguing with Coke about Black truck drivers. There were always two people on a Coca-Cola truck, and the driver was in charge. He sold the Cokes and wrote the receipts, and the Black guy lifted the heavy cases of Coke off of the truck and took them into the store, bar, club, or wherever they were going. The driver was always white. And the driver made at least three times more than the other guy. So, one of our first battles was to get Coke to hire Black drivers for the delivery trucks. It seems like an awfully irrelevant, simple thing now, but at that time it was a monumental step to get Black drivers.

In Mobile, Alabama, we had a terrible struggle with a supermarket, Delchamps. It was the big boy in Mobile, and we tried to get the owner to hire a Black cashiers. All of this was a struggle to democratize capitalism, and we had one heck of a time getting Delchamps to hire Black cashiers who wrote the receipts and kept up with the sales and made the money.

So this struggle to democratize capitalism—or to move from civil rights to silver rights—is an old struggle that needs to be invigorated and reinvigorated, for this disparity is a significant part of our struggle that is yet to catch up. The criminal justice system hasn't even heard yet that there's a movement to democratize capitalism in America. At least the corporate structure has heard about it. They haven't conformed as they ought to, but they've heard about it.

In Georgia, Blacks constitute about 30 percent of the general population. But we really don't know how many Blacks are in Georgia or anywhere else for that matter. White folks cannot count Black people, and Black people will not cooperate. When the census is taken, Black folk are suspicious of anybody with a necktie, a pencil, and some paper asking questions. But out of the general population with 30 percent of blacks in Georgia, more than 66 percent of the prison population is African American. And that's not unrelated to the military, prison, or industrial makeup regarding African Americans in this country.

There seems to be an ulterior relationship with our economic justice problem. Even today, with all of the progress we've made in integration, African Americans' income level lingers around 60 percent of the average income of whites. It's a Herculean task to try to overcome the disparity. At the policy level, we continue to work with the private sector to put African Americans and other people of color on corporate boards because that's where the policies are established. And we work to get the private sector to integrate at the management level so that when executive decisions are made, Blacks are there to make sure policies are carried out. The problem lies at the policy level, and that's where the rubber meets the road. We work with the public sector to establish guidelines for the private sector.

Our minimum wage in this country is profane. And when we say what it is, it's like we're cussing. How we expect families to live on minimum wage is a mystery to me. The minimum wage is a form of persistent oppression in this country, and the struggle for silver rights must take it into account.

We must put the issue of economics in the proper theological and spiritual context. It is not a secular issue. Nothing is sacred *or* secular. All life and all aspects of life are sacred. My Bible doesn't say that *portions* of the earth belong to the Lord. But the earth is the Lord's; the cattle on a thousand hills and the oil—it doesn't belong to Texaco, or Halliburton and Cheney—belong to God. And we must see the assets that God has provided his universe. We must see our obligation as sacred and see that assets are equitably distributed. I've stopped using the word *equally,* and I use *equitably* instead.

I'm reminded of a story of an old farmer in south Georgia who made what he called rabbit sausage and he darn near got rich doing it. People who didn't eat pork bought it. But then rabbits became scarce. He had a problem and didn't know what to do. So the farmer started using horses instead of rabbits and continued to call it rabbit sausage. But somebody snitched on him to the feds, and they objected to him calling it rabbit sausage because he was using horse meat along with whatever rabbits he could find. They evaluated the product and told the farmer he was misleading the public. The farmer disagreed and stood firm on the fact that the ingredients were equal. The inspectors told the farmer that he might avoid trouble if the ingredients were indeed equal. So they questioned him about the amounts he used in making the sausage, and he assured the inspectors the ingredients were equal. The farmer confirmed, "Every time I put in one rabbit, I put in one horse."

That's why I've stopped using the word *equal,* because even though it's equal, it ain't equitable! We must look at America's economic life and her structures from the perspective of equity, not just equality. The new translations of the Bible do not speak of charity; they speak of love. The Bible speaks of faith, hope, and love, and the greatest of these is love. And love is expressed in justice, and justice includes economic justice. Love is inclusive, and that's why we need to move from civil rights to silver rights.

CHAPTER SIX

IT'S TIME TO MOVE TO ANOTHER MOUNTAIN

You have moved around this mountain long enough! Go northward!
—Deuteronomy 2:3 (paraphrase)

Mountains hold mystique; they capture the hearts and minds of us mortals. There is a lure of heights. I suppose, in part, it seems "heavenward." Dangers also lurk there. I carried three grandkids to the Smokies a couple of summers ago. We had a great time with—among other things—bears. The mountains fascinate us. Whether it's the Rockies or the Sierras in the West; the Blue Ridge in Appalachia in the South; the Alps in Europe; the Andes in South America; Kilimanjaro in Africa; or even Stone Mountain in Georgia, mountains have been and remain imposing factors in human experience.

In the text, the children of Israel were on a pilgrimage from Egypt to Canaan. They seemed to have settled into a plateau of contentment too far from Canaan. How far? Too far! They had grown too satisfied with the status quo. In context of the movement, we have let tokenism substitute for authentic inclusiveness. Apathy, complacency, and intellectual, physical, and spiritual de-escalation are problematic. Our comfort zones have become stagnant. There's no excitement about moving on up a little higher. No enthusiasm about outreach and sharing and expanding our sense of mission. You have been on this mountain long enough. It is time to move from this mountain.

To the men of our tribe, here is the challenge: You have been on this level long enough. This plateau of tokenism, this hillside of partialism—you are halfway up and have confused this point with the peak. It's time to move from the molehill to the mountaintop.

As we look analytically and empirically at this present age, we can rejoice at much we see. Our technology, our scientific advancement, is incredible. The recent advances in genetics—the genome has excited the world of medical technology like nothing I have seen in my lifetime, even surpassing the miracles related to heart surgery. We continue to move higher and higher in this discipline.

But we are stuck on the same old mountain in human relations and racial justice. It's time to match our technological advancement with sociological advancement and theological understanding. With all the glorious opportunities for longer and healthier lives, we continue to poison the streams of our present and future with prejudice, bias, hatred, greed, violence, materialism, classism, racism, sexism. With all the riches poured into human experience, we continue to experience the plagues of poverty: homelessness, crimes, overcrowded prisons. It is time to move from this mountain.

It's time for the nation to move to another mountain. Long before September 11, 2001, we were on course for disaster with growing, widening disparities in income. Class divisions are threatening our "united" status. It is time to move from the mountain of insensitivity to the least of these; from the mountain of intolerance of those who are different; from the disparities between those who have more than they will ever need and those who never have as much as they always need; from the molehill of minimum wage to the mountain of livable wage. I am tired of minimum: minimum health care, minimum health, minimum car, minimum house, minimum hug, minimum kiss, minimum rest. Move from minimum to adequate, even from the concept of equality to equity. In the community of faith we have begun to tolerate disparities. It's time to move from the hill of charity to the mountain of love.

There are forces attempting to redefine the nation in their own image, particularly in the mold of economic elitism. Our nation has had some great and defining moments: Bill of Rights; Gettysburg Address; Emancipation Proclamation; Boston Tea Party; women's suffrage; voting rights and 1954 Supreme Court decision; 1964 Public Accommodations Act; collective bargaining; emergence of public transit.

It is time to move from insensitivity to the critical nature of transportation as a technical and spiritual connecting force that can bring us together. A few years ago I joined Rod Slater, Secretary of Transportation in the Clinton cabinet, and officials of the Transit Association in presenting the Rosa Parks award, a symbol of the nation moving from the mountain of discrimination in transportation to higher ground. The boycott of buses was the birth of self-determination and revelation of the significance of public (people's) transit. The transit system satisfied a vital need—connecting. People stayed off buses in Montgomery because everyone who had ever ridden or had relatives who had, directly or vicariously experienced the humiliation of Rosa Parks. People's transit was a common denominator.

We are going through a crisis over raising fares on MARTA (Metropolitan Atlanta Rapid Transit Authority). Some professor was engaged as a consultant to inform us that an increase in fares would negatively impact low-income transit dependent riders, reaffirming what we already knew.

It's time to call upon elected officials and politicians to move from the mountain of opportunistic exploitation and stop just decrying the need for adjustment in the fare at a time of crisis. The time to deal with an issue is before the crisis arises, before the roof starts leaking. Of course, management must leave no stone unturned, no corner of costs unexamined and subject to be cut until they can cut no more. The board has every right and responsibility to demand that management assure that every austere measure that can be taken is taken to maintain affordable

> LOWERY SERVED ON THE MARTA BOARD FOR TWENTY-FOUR YEARS, FOUR OF THOSE AS ITS CHAIR. HE FOUGHT CONSTANTLY FOR MINORITIES TO GET MAJOR CONTRACTS AND TO KEEP THE FARES LOW SO TRANSPORTATION WOULD ALWAYS BE AFFORDABLE FOR LOW-INCOME CITIZENS.

fares. The basic and sacred purpose of people's transit is defeated if those who need it most can afford it least.

If, however, we are forced to reduce services, the purpose is frustrated, so there must be a combined campaign between public and private sectors in Metro Atlanta to find additional resources so that MARTA will not only refuse to reduce service but can expand service and maintain affordable fares.

A community that can continue to build multi-million-dollar arenas and stadiums ought to find ways to build greater and more affordable people's transit. There is something wrong with our leadership in government and business if we can house entertainment but cannot house the homeless—if we can spend billions in facilities for entertainment, then additional millions for salaries, and then additional costs for traffic direction—but cannot produce necessary resources for effective, efficient, affordable public transit. We clearly need to move to a higher mountain.

When our governmental leaders shoot from the hip and lip and not from the heart and soul in response to a cry for help from the people's transit, they ignore the vital role that transportation has played. Our system in the mid-1990s moved a half million persons a day. We had to find a way to move twenty-five million people in seventeen days during the Olympics.

Perhaps we need to call upon the governor and GRTA (Georgia Regional Transportation Authority) to create an alliance between the public and private sectors to come up with resources from every possible level to improve and expand public transportation and forever maintain affordable fares for transit-dependent people.

In health, it's time to move from a mountain where forty million persons in this nation have no health insurance. It's time to move and redefine health care so that adequate, affordable care is available to all our citizens. Where is the universal character, the ethical mandate in the genome, if millions cannot afford the benefits of our divine gifts? It's time to move from the mountain of placing medical judgments in the hands of nonmedical personnel.

It's time to move from inequity to equity in education. Understand the trickery in the scheme of vouchers that have some appeal to desperate parents, but look at the whole. From molehill of self first to mountain of community, vouchers are a scheme to favor the few, lead to disintegration of public schools, and help shape values and priorities. We have trouble finding resources for public schools because our values and priorities are at levels of molehills instead of mountains. When we want new stadiums or arenas for entertainment, we find resources, tear down stadiums not yet paid for, and build new ones with plush boxes for the fat, while cardboard boxes sit under bridges for the poor and homeless. While on the subject of education, we must move from molehill to mountain in the misconception that it is not black for our young men to be smart. There is no substitute for hard work.

In the criminal justice system, it's time to move from mole hill to mountain. The criminal justice system of 2001 is more like that of 1901. We Black people are one of three in the population, but more than two of three in prisons—most with inadequate or no defense. Three strikes and you're out. In Georgia, thanks to Zell Miller, it's two strikes. We are filling our prisons because of disparities in sentencing. One of every four young men is in trouble. And now this issue includes young women.

Finally, we need twenty-first-century activists—new millennium movers and shakers—as we seek to move to the mountaintop. We must believe that faith can move mountains, but faith without works is dead. Once we were activists and mountains were shaken and negative forces trembled before our unity and righteousness. Come now. We've been on this hill too long. When we met with President Lyndon Johnson following the passage of the Public Accommodations Act, we declared that we must now pursue the right to vote. He said it was too soon, but we had waited long enough. We went back to the drawing board and planned the Selma to Montgomery campaign. We wrote the Voting Rights Act and carried it back to the president who drawled on TV that "we shall overcome."

We must be reenergized. You can't imagine Einstein without math and physics; Disney World without Mickey Mouse; Rome without the Colosseum; Duke Ellington without "Satin Doll"; Ray Charles without "Georgia on My Mind"; Aretha without

"Respect"; Ali without "float like a butterfly, sting like a bee"; Mahalia without "Move on Up a Little Higher." So, how can you imagine the movement getting to this point, not being reenergized, and continuing to move to higher mountains? It's time for us to move a little higher. It's time to move off this mountain. We have been here too long. It's time to move to higher ground.

CHAPTER SEVEN

STIR WHAT YOU'VE GOT

Cascade United Methodist Church, Atlanta, Georgia, Late 1980s

*The husbandman that laboureth must be first
partaker of the fruits.* —2 Timothy 2:6

What Paul told Timothy in his second letter was this: "Timothy, I know you are wrestling with some problems, but I want to remind you to stir up the gifts of God that I know are within you." A lot of us are like Timothy: worried about what we don't have when we are not using what we do have. God has given us what we need. Just stir up what you've got.

Paul was really referring to Timothy's ordination, but his message is too broad to limit it to just Timothy's ordination. This applies to all who have walked down the aisle to give God your heart and the preacher your hand. It applies to all of us. Stir up what God has put in you. Don't let that baptismal fire you got when you joined the church die out. Don't let the fire simmer down to a flickering flame, growing weak and dim from negative winds of doubt from within and from without. You

IN 1986, REV. JOSEPH LOWERY BECAME THE EIGHTEENTH PASTOR OF CASCADE UNITED METHODIST CHURCH IN ATLANTA. DURING HIS PASTORATE THE MEMBERSHIP GREW AND SO DID THE WORSHIP FACILITY. NOTING THE IMPORTANCE OF EDUCATION FOR GENERATIONS AFTER THE CIVIL RIGHTS MOVEMENT, THE CONGREGATION ESTABLISHED SEVERAL SCHOLARSHIP PROGRAMS FOR GRADE SCHOOL AND COLLEGE-BOUND STUDENTS. REV. LOWERY RETIRED AS SENIOR PASTOR IN 1992; HE CONTINUES TO WORSHIP AT CASCADE.

cannot let the flame die down because you didn't keep the fire refueled. You don't expect your car to go on forever without refueling. So when God fills up your tank, it doesn't mean that you never have to do anything else. We must understand more theology so that we will know that even when we are born again, in order to keep running, we must come back from time to time to fill up. We must be rekindled. Newer translations use the phrase "rekindle your gifts." I still like "stir up your gifts." We have to stir up our commitment to Christ with prayer, worship, and unceasing service.

Paul is saying to us that there is stuff in us that we don't know we have. But there is another lesson in this text. Paul is suggesting that all of us have some gifts that we are only partially using. Ordinary people have some physical strength that they never use. Remember the old TV show *The Incredible Hulk*? The Hulk was an ordinary person until something stirred within him and ignited his extraordinary strength. It is the same thing with us. When you stir up what is inside you, you gain new strength.

I'll give you another example. This small, fragile lady was looking out of her window at her husband working on his car when suddenly the jack slipped and the car came crashing down on his chest. She screamed and ran to him and lifted the car from him. When he crawled out safely, she fainted. Now, she rose to the occasion by stirring up what was within her. She didn't even know she had that kind of strength.

There is stuff within you that, if you use it, you don't know what you might be able to do. Let God challenge you. Stop worrying about what you can't do or don't have. Don't worry that you can't sing like Marian Anderson or play ball like Jackie Robinson or preach like great preachers. Say something sweet to someone who might need an encouraging word. Use what you have.

Stir up your intellectual energy. You just don't know how much brain power you have. I've read that we use only 24 to 33 percent of our brains. Let God stir up your intellectual energy and see what you might be able to accomplish. Some of us have physical energy, some of us have intellectual energy, and some of us are lazy spiritually. Our spiritual energy must undergird all that we are and all that we do. Without a true relationship with God in Christ Jesus we are in trouble. Stir up what you've got so that you can be all that you can be in God's army. The eye can't say to the ear: I don't need you; neither can the hand say that to the leg. All parts of the body are important in the body of Christ. Likewise, every talent is important. Spiritual energy needs to be stirred up. God gives us what is needed to build us, not destroy us; to enlarge, not to belittle; to inspire, not to be mean or demean.

Paul reminded Timothy of who he was and where he came from. Paul told Timothy that he knew his grandmother, Lois, and his mother, Eunice. They had good stuff in them, so Timothy came from good stock. He just needed to rekindle and stir it up.

Some of what they had must be in you. Paul is talking to us all today. We have a grand heritage. Our forefathers withstood tough times and accomplished much. They stirred up their gifts and stood firm in the storm. They didn't have sturdy ships like we have now, but they stood the storm. They didn't have the medical advantages that we have, but they stood the storm. Their cold was colder, their nights longer; but their faith was bolder. They cried out, "Father, I stretch my hands to Thee. No other help I know." Our ancestors stirred up their gifts and made it a mighty long way.

We carry things much too long. We carry grudges and bitter fruit, not understanding that this does us more harm than good. The person you are angry with and holding the grudge against has probably let it go and moved on while you are still holding on. Letting go of some of that hatred is better than a dose of Pepto-Bismol!

Stir up your gifts. Stir some forgiveness in your heart. It will build a lining around your heart and will lighten the burden you're carrying. Stir up determination. Determine to try it God's way by trying love and trying forgiveness. Stir up your giving. Just try giving more to the church, and watch how God blesses you. Stir up love and devotion, and show love to those who appear to be unlovable. Stir up grace. There is no secret what God can do when you stir up the gifts that are within you.

I was having tea with a friend, and I didn't remember putting sugar in the cup. It was still bitter when I took my first sip. Before

I could add sugar, my friend reminded me that I had already added the sugar and that it probably was at the bottom of the cup. When I checked, sure enough, there was the sugar. I just needed to stir it up. When I did, I could taste the sweetness, and it was good to the last drop. That's the way God needs us to be. He needs us to stir up what he has already deposited in us. Look somewhere down at the bottom of your dedication. It's there! Stir up prayer. Stir up worship. Stir up unceasing service. Whatever you have within you, stir it up!

CHAPTER EIGHT

"THE AMEN CORNER": TIME FOR NATIONAL REPENTANCE; TIME FOR HEALING[1]

1999

All have sinned and fallen short. —Romans 3:23 (paraphrase)

William Jefferson Clinton has a weak streak in his being that stands in the need of prayer and grace. Kenneth Starr has a mean streak in his being that also stands in the need of prayer and grace. "The Amen Corner" will not attempt to defend the president, for his behavior is indefensible and reprehensible. A man of Clinton's intellectual prowess, not to mention common sense, should yield not to temptation no matter how aggressively proffered by a flirtatious, giddy intern. To attempt to negotiate a perilous tightrope (that only partially defines the Lewinsky affair) after surviving the Gennifer Flowers and Paula Jones minefields is both foolhardy and arrogant. The president has confessed his sins, asked for forgiveness, and promised to go and sin no more. He and his family have been through the very bowels of hell. Enough already.

Now, someone ought to exhort Kenneth Starr to confess and repent for his transgressions, his persecutorial rather than prosecutorial behavior. He typifies forces that have tried to destroy Clinton from day one, *by any means necessary....* When they struck out on Whitewater and the other criminal charges, they went to bat to find hits in his private sex life. Starr should have rejected the garbage dumped in his lap by mercenary Linda Tripp. The Paula Jones case, which triggered much of the assault, has been dismissed. To add contempt to insult, Judge Starr submits a pornographic report obviously designed to humiliate and devastate the president and his family. Now it appears on the Internet for all our children to view. Congress is determined to upstage *Penthouse* as a porn publisher.

Unfortunately, the president's weakness and the special persecutor's meanness are signs of our times. We have tolerated weakness and celebrated meanness. Our culture has been wounded by moral compromise and political violence. So, Clinton and Starr are mirrors of us—arrogance of power, unbridled vindictiveness, *pleasure and profit by any means.* Where have all the principles, noble and mighty, gone? Long time passing. Where has all the compassion gone? Long time passing. We are still groping for meaning in a new and undefined era. The Cold War hysteria era has passed, but during that era, we sacrificed principle, compromised ideals, minimized honor, maximized opportunism, exalted materialism, demonized the saints, and canonized the devil—all in the name of fighting the evil empire. We have sown the wind and we are reaping the whirlwind. We have deserted the good spouse of spirituality and we are carrying on an affair with the prostitute of materialism and greed. It is an incestuous affair and produces offspring with the congenital defects of economic exploitation, sexual exploitation, racism, sexism, gun addiction, drug addiction, pleasure, and profit by any means necessary. We need a revival of spirituality, of values and plain old devotion to truth and high moral principles. Our perception of morality must extend beyond sex. Moral authority, for the president, includes the capacity to lead the nation to address *hunger, health care, quality education, and peace and justice.*

Our challenge is to seek a resolution that serves the best interest of the nation, not a political party, or Congress, or the White House. The first step needs to be a national act of repentance. We have all sinned. "The Amen Corner" does not believe impeachment or resignation can serve the best interest of the nation. The president can be stronger, the nation can be kinder and gentler, and we can all be purged of selfishness and be baptized in grace and forgiveness. *Healing* of the nation can begin.

Finally, so many people have expressed alarm at the media frenzy surrounding this crisis. Senator Joseph Lieberman in a brilliant, if ill-timed, statement frightened us when he said no president can ever again have privacy because of news media standards. Columnist Anthony Lewis goes a step further and asks: Can the president ever have confidential talks with advisers? Are Secret Service personnel doomed to be spies or witnesses? Who in the world will seek office under those circumstances? Privacy in our lives is as necessary as water. Lewis also quotes NYU professor of philosophy and law Thomas Nagel who wrote that *each of our inner lives is such a jungle of thoughts, feelings, fantasies and impulses that civilization would be impossible if we expressed them all... social life would be impossible if we expressed all our lustful, aggressive, greedy, anxious or self-obsessed feelings in ordinary public encounters, so would inner life be impossible if we tried to become wholly persons whose thoughts, feelings and private behavior could be safely exposed to public view.* In addition, look at how we reward those who take it upon themselves to confess other people's wrongs and indiscretions—in books and everywhere.

Let us pray that the Republican (Gingrich) strategy of releasing more and more damaging materials (inundation) will not prevail and compel the nation to suffer the trauma of the process of impeachment or resignation.

A great hymn contains a verse that reads:

When through fiery trials thy pathways shall lie,
My grace, all sufficient, shall be thy supply;
The flame shall not hurt thee;
I only design thy dross to consume, and thy gold to refine.

The "Corner" concludes with a line from the Lord's Prayer: **Forgive us our trespasses as we forgive those who trespass against us. Let the church say *Amen*!**

NOTE

1. "The Amen Corner" is a column written for the National Newspaper Press Association (NNPA). This one was written in the heat of the Clinton-Lewinsky affair.

CHAPTER NINE

RESPECT: A MATRIX FOR SPIRITUALITY

Georgia Day, National Cathedral, Washington, D.C., November 2001

*Then he answered and spake unto me, saying, This is the word of the
Lord unto Zerubbabel, saying, Not by might, nor by power, but by my
spirit, saith the Lord of hosts.* —Zechariah 4:6

*When the Son of man shall come in his glory, and all the holy angels
with him, then shall he sit upon the throne of his glory:
And before him shall be gathered all nations: and he shall separate
them one from another, as a shepherd divideth his sheep from the
goats: And he shall set the sheep on his right hand,
but the goats on the left.
Then shall the King say unto them on his right hand, Come, ye blessed
of my Father, inherit the kingdom prepared for you
from the foundation of the world:
For I was ahungered, and ye gave me meat: I was thirsty, and ye gave
me drink: I was a stranger, and ye took me in:....
And the King shall answer and say unto them, Verily I say unto you,
Inasmuch as ye have done it unto one of the least of these my brethren,
ye have done it unto me.* —Matthew 25:31-35, 40

Earlier this year, I had the privilege of speaking at a conference
of mayors in Savannah, the port city of the state of Georgia.
That evening, I heard, in the dimness between sleep and being
awake, a report on some group's assessment of the greatest one
hundred songs of the last century. Number one was "Over the
Rainbow"; number two was "White Christmas"; number three
was "This Land Is Your Land"; and number four was "Respect."
When this song became a hit in 1967, many believed it was a banner song for women's rights. I just think Aretha Franklin had a
way of saying and singing that a woman wants to be treated right

by the man in her life. Incidentally, that song was written by Otis Redding, who was from the state of Georgia.

In more than a half century of ministry, I have married many couples. Usually in counseling sessions with the couple, I play a little game. I ask them to choose one word they would like to see as a dynamic in their relationship. At the top of the list is *love*. Not far behind is *trust*. They toss about other terms and finally arrive at *respect*. I've concluded that nothing is more important than respect. Beloved, we are the sons and daughters of God. There is sacredness in our very being. No one has the right to abuse or misuse or neglect.

Vows are a commitment to aid in each other's fulfillment of the promise. If I could have, I would have had Otis Redding try *reverence* as the subject of his song. After making an attempt to rewrite music history and testing out my replacement in the lyrics, it didn't really work for me. Even for a seasoned preacher, it was a losing battle trying to compete with the Queen of Soul and the genius of Otis Redding. But inherent in this word *respect* is *revere*. The genesis of self-respect is knowing who you are and never letting others define you. There is no need to debate the identity of Jesus. He defined himself clearly for us in the text.

America has many defining moments. You might even consider them as vows—like the Boston Tea Party, the Declaration of Independence, the Emancipation Proclamation, the Bill of Rights, the 1954 Supreme Court ruling of *Brown v. The Board of Education,* the Civil Rights Act of 1964, and the Voting Rights Act of 1965. These are all moments in our history that have shaped and defined us as a nation. These events were vows America made to its citizens. There are those who think other events hold a special place in history. During the fiftieth anniversary of the film *Gone with the Wind,* a reporter from *USA Today* called me to get my thoughts on what he viewed as a defining moment in our country. I had to rephrase Rhett Butler's famous line in the movie and tell the reporter that, frankly, I didn't put too much stock in his definition of this anniversary as a defining moment in history. Too much has been sacrificed to ensure our rights, so I am not quick to get caught up in romanticizing interpretations of dark times in our history.

In Christ we are empowered to define ourselves. Through him, we are born again. Many parents take great care in selecting names for their children. They look for names on which their children can stand, names that will help usher these young ones into their destinies. Look at the name Augustine, originating from Caesar Augustus. It means "grand" or "majestic." I'm glad my parents chose to name me Joseph; it means "May God give increase." And then we examine the name of our Savior—the Messiah—which means "deliverer." There is power in this name! So along this same line of thought, your name ought to mean something; it should elicit respect. Your name helps define you, and it lets others know who you are.

Respect allows us to better relate to the world around us. It is a way of being that opens us up to the awe and splendor of God's universe while giving reverence to the Creator.

The Creator, the creatures, and creation. The respect for each of these should be thought of as a matrix for spirituality. Creation empowers us to respect the sacredness of our being and the sacredness of others. It allows us to relate to each other in God's creation, not for what they can do for us but for who we are and who they are. As members of the body of Christ, we are called to embody the divine energy that is loose in the universe. To deny this embodiment of divine intent is to abandon the good spouse of spirituality and cohabit with the prostitute of materialism and greed, producing offspring with congenital defects of racism, sexism, greed and economic exploitation, addiction to guns, and addiction to sex. Denial leads to marketplace mentality, which is knowing the price of everything but understanding the value of nothing. Reverence for the Creator, the creatures, and creation leads us to become instruments of healing for the distortions in our social, economic, and political institutions.

Spirituality empowers us to become part and parcel of the solutions rather than the problems. A lack of spirituality leads to economic elitism and the growing disparities that breed social disruption. Spirituality calls us to seriously address the disparities between those who have more than they'll ever need and those who have less than they always need.

The spirituality I'm speaking of is a new level of reverence for life and the living. This spirituality will take us beyond declaring war on the terrorists to waging fierce battles against the political, social, and economic factors that breed terrorism. Make no mistake. There is no justification for the madness that we have seen, but respect provides opportunity to take the moral high ground in bringing these culprits to justice.

In a sense, we are caught in a war between fear and hope. Fear will drive us to seek security through vengeance and violence. But faith calls us to work through international bodies of law and justice to not only bring perpetrators to justice but to contribute to building a world wherein understanding the sacredness of all God's children will guide and shape our economic, social, and political policies and practices.

The community of faith must raise serious questions about whether we can sustain our existence as an island of doing well when we are surrounded by a world that is hungry, naked, sick, and imprisoned in cells of hopelessness and desperation. Hope can win! Weeping may endure for a night, but hold on. When hope unborn had died, we held on to hope anyway. Joy cometh in the morning! Even when we sang the blues, we had hope in the core of our souls: "I'm blue but I won't be blue always. The sun's going to shine in my back door someday." But of course, our hope is built on a higher level: "I'm so glad trouble don't last always," and "My hope is built on nothing less than Jesus' blood and righteousness."

Will defeat in war or even the death of terrorists bring lasting peace? Or should we cry out, "Only triumph through spirituality and respect for humanity will last!"

We have a glimpse of who we are as sons and daughters of the Creator in daring, loving rescue efforts and a sense of oneness in the human family. That is our real spiritual identity. Therein are the genuine patriotism and spirituality that will lead to and define patriotism at the highest level. Just as we rescued our brothers and sisters from the tragic rubble in noble and vast dimensions, let us rescue the unemployed with health benefits and have blessed assurance wrapped in meaningful insurance. Patriotism that is born out of spirituality will lead us to the re-creation of and the retraining for jobs and to health care. Respect for one another can lead us to the blessing of our civil liberties, not the destruction of those principles that have brought us to the edge of greatness.

In chapter 20 of 1 Kings, Benhadad, from his evil vantage point, cries that the Israelites' God will not save them in the next battle because their god is a god of the hills. His army would fight the Israelites in the plains. But Benhadad didn't know the God of Ahab! He is God of the hills and plains, great and small, rich and poor, North and South, Black and white, gay and straight, streets and suites, Afghanistan and Atlanta, Pakistan and Pittsburgh. Our victory in personal, social, and political battles is connected to the respect we have for God and for one another!

CHAPTER TEN

HEED THEIR RISING VOICES

A group of outstanding citizens purchased an ad in the *New York Times* on March 7, 1960, to raise funds to support the movement in Alabama. They called it "Heed Their Rising Voices," and it was signed by such outstanding figures as Eleanor Roosevelt, Sammy Davis, Jr., Harry Belafonte, Reinhold Niebuhr, and others. They were loyal and enthusiastic supporters of the movement and the ad was severely critical of the Montgomery City Commissioners and the Governor, John Patterson. It accused them of persecuting the students and ministers leading the movement.

The City Commissioner, L. B. Sullivan, the Governor, and other city officials filed libel suits against the *New York Times* and the Alabama ministers: Ralph Abernathy, Joseph Lowery, Fred Shuttlesworth, and Solomon Seay. They actually won judgments against us. The commissioners executed the judgment, and while the *New York Times* posted bond pending appeal, we could not raise bond, and our personal properties were seized. Fred, Solomon, and I owned cars, but they discovered land in Marengo County, Alabama, and seized farms of the Abernathy family.

In Mobile, they took my

NEW YORK TIMES CO. V. SULLIVAN IS THE 1964 CASE DECIDED BY THE U.S. SUPREME COURT REGARDING ACTUAL MALICE. IN 1963, THE STATE OF ALABAMA FILED A SUIT CITING LIBEL AGAINST FOUR MINISTERS—REV. JOSEPH LOWERY, REV. RALPH ABERNATHY, REV. S. S. SEAY, AND REV. FRED SHUTTLESWORTH IN RESPONSE TO A FULL-PAGE AD THAT RAN IN THE NEW YORK TIMES. THE STATE WON ITS CASE BUT THE SUPREME COURT OVERTURNED THE RULING.

car, a Chrysler. I will never forget the sight of my three daughters crying in the doorway of the parsonage as the wrecker towed the car away. A few weeks later, they sold my car at an auction for less than nine hundred dollars. The good news was that it was purchased by R. B. DeWitt, a YMCA executive and member of my congregation. He sold our car to my wife for one dollar! The community reimbursed DeWitt.

The case was appealed to the U.S. Supreme Court, which reversed the Alabama court's decision and issued a landmark ruling favoring the ministers and the *New York Times*. The ruling was written by Justice William Brennan. Justice Black of Alabama wrote that unless there was malice, it was difficult to libel a public official. In his book *Make No Law,* Anthony Lewis said that this is the classic ruling on libel.

The trial, held in Montgomery, was typical of the justice system in America, particularly the South. The lawyers for Sullivan found occasion to call Sammy Davis's name as often as possible. He had recently married a white blonde named May Britt, and his name was poison to some whites in the Deep South. Every time Sammy Davis's name was called, a good ol' boy's face would light up. The lawyer for Sullivan said, "These preachers are sitting here with an air of injured innocence when they are secretly proud to have their names listed with Eleanor Roosevelt, Harry Belafonte, and Sammy Davis, Jr." The deliberation didn't take long; the judgment for five hundred thousand dollars took only about two hours. The reversal by the Supreme Court was argued in January 1964 and decided in March 1964. Our hope was in the Supreme Court, which ruled in our favor 9-0.

The *New York Times* posted a supersedeas bond and therefore was not subject to the seizure of property. They would not let us be covered under their bond. Too much risk, they said, since we were residents of Alabama. Thanks a lot!

Prior to the 1964 ruling, states determined what was considered libelous. This landmark case established the criteria that would be used nationwide when determining libel cases involving public officials. Oh, glory!

CHAPTER ELEVEN

THE ESSENCE AND QUINTESSENCE OF AFRICAN MANHOOD: NELSON MANDELA

Big Bethel Baptist Church, Atlanta, Georgia, 1990

Understandably, our deputy president has expended a tremendous amount of energy. We don't want to keep him any longer than we have to, but, Mr. Chairman, Mr. Deputy President. Your Worship—where is Your Worship? Mandela had called Maynard Jackson, our mayor, "Your Worship." That means that from this day forward, his behavior must be impeccable. Mr. Ambassador Young, Mrs. King, it is my privilege as co-chair of this occasion and chair of the civil human rights celebration to call to order this historic assemblage. We are here to receive our hero! We are here to hail the fact that the struggle for racial and economic justice is a global struggle. Our distinguished guest puts flesh and blood on the international character of the struggle against apartheid in South Africa and against the apartheid mentality in south Georgia and south Philadelphia and south Chicago and south everywhere!

We welcome you to Atlanta, and let me set the record straight since this is the home of nonviolence. I want to address the questions they keep posing to Mr. Mandela about violence. We, who are thoroughly committed to the efficacy of nonviolence, nevertheless respect the right of oppressed people everywhere to seek their liberation within the context of their own sensitivity. Furthermore, we in this nation, when did we become so concerned about violence? We are they, who funded the Contras to slay innocent people in Central America. We are they, who with violence invaded Panama and left thousands homeless and dead and crippled. Who are we to raise the question of violence? And not only that, but to this day, we are funding UNITA and Jonas Savimbi, the flunkies of P. W. Botha and F. W. deKlerk, who are killing people in Angola. Who are we to raise the question of violence?

Here in this nonviolent movement headquarters, we recognize the fact that in our struggle, our Constitution guarantees our rights while the South African government guarantees "wrong." There is a conscience in this country to which we can appeal. There was no conscience in the South African government. We're here to say, Mr. President, we pledge our continued support as you process triumphantly from the prison in South Africa with your head high, your spirit undaunted, your mind sharp, without bitterness. You are the essence and quintessence of African manhood; we salute you! And so we say, Mr. Deputy President, march on. Our movement is from Selma to Soweto, from Birmingham to Berlin, from Montgomery to Manila, from Ireland to our land, from Los Angeles to Angola, and from Jackson to Johannesburg.

We shall never turn back. We've come too far, marched too long, prayed too hard, wept too bitterly, bled too profusely, and died too young to let anybody turn back the clock. We ain't going back . . . we're going forward.

So after the death of our first president, Martin Luther King, Jr., in 1968, the Board of Directors of the Southern Christian Leadership Conference established the Martin Luther King, Jr., Award. There are many other awards—one of them is particularly important and significant—but they all come after this award. And today, we are pleased to give the Martin Luther King, Jr., Human Rights Award to a man who has stood for twenty-seven years, unquivering, with-

UNITA IS THE SECOND LARGEST POLITICAL PARTY IN ANGOLA. FOR YEARS, THE NATIONALIST GROUP WAGED WAR AGAINST PORTUGUESE AND ANGOLAN FORCES. THE PARTY RECEIVED FUNDING FROM THE UNITED STATES AND SOUTH AFRICA AND WAS LED BY JONAS SAVIMBI FROM 1966 UNTIL HIS DEATH IN 2002.

out compromise, and without bitterness. He refused to come out of jail when they said, "All you've got to do is denounce violence, and you can come out of jail." He said, "Until my people are free, until they have the rights guaranteed them by God and this country's nobility, though hidden in apartheid, I will not come out."

Mr. Nelson Mandela, we award you the 1990 Martin Luther King, Jr., Human Rights Award.

CHAPTER TWELVE

TOMMY LEE HINES:
A CLASS FOR THE KLAN

On May 26, 1979, we traveled to Decatur, Alabama, for a march in defense of Tommy Lee Hines, a twenty-five-year-old mentally challenged man convicted by an all-white jury for the rape of a white woman. The police story had Tommy fleeing the rape scene in a car. Tommy was not even capable of riding a bicycle. His mental age was around six years.

R. B. Cottonreader, of our staff, had been monitoring the situation and was keeping us advised of the racial tension that the trial and situation had created in Decatur. We needed to show the citizens that we cared and not allow them to feel isolated and without support.

When we got to the church, Cottonreader told us of reports on CB radios of Klansmen discussing plans to "get Lowery and Nettles" and others. We called the state troopers and apprised them of these threats, but they did not respond. There were some who felt that the situation was too volatile and that the march should be postponed. We prayed and deliberated over the situation and knew that marching was our only option. We could not allow the Klan to line the streets of Decatur and intimidate the community any more than it already had. The community all knew Tommy and that he was not capable of committing any of these crimes. He had been railroaded. So we decided to march.

Evelyn usually marches beside me, but I thought better of that on this day and insisted that she drive our car behind the marchers. There were around two hundred marchers with us. We left from the church, singing and praying. As we rounded the corner toward downtown, the Klan was waiting for us with billy clubs and guns. They shot at the first line of marchers. As bullets flew over my head, our marshals immediately lifted me from where I was standing and away from the line of fire.

What about Evelyn? What about Evelyn? The Klan moved swiftly past the marchers and straight to my car that Evelyn was driving and fired two shots into the windshield, barely missing her. She dropped down onto the seat to protect herself as best she could. She could hear the Klansmen talking, calling each other by their first names. Knowing she could not remain there indefinitely, she decided to look up, and if the road was clear, she would take off. It was, and she did. Somehow she found her way back to the church. With glass shattered all over her and the front seat of the car, she made her way inside, shaking.

Four brave young marchers received gunshot wounds that day, but thanks be to God, no injuries were very serious.

We returned to Decatur, Alabama, three weeks later with buses and church vans galore from all over the country—ten thousand strong. The Klan showed up, too, but this time the march remained nonviolent under the watchful eyes of hundreds of officers.

Tommy's conviction was reversed by the state court in 1980.

There was a federal investigation, but nothing came of it. Morris Dees of the Southern Poverty Law Center in Montgomery filed a federal lawsuit against Klansmen known to have been involved. Almost a decade later, six Klansmen received federal sentences and were fined. To reduce their sentences, they could attend a class on race relations with me as the instructor. One of them declined, calling it "cruel and unusual punishment."

When the media got wind of the class, they wanted to

> THE SOUTHERN POVERTY LAW CENTER IS A NONPROFIT CIVIL RIGHTS ORGANIZATION THAT WAS ESTABLISHED IN 1971 WITH THE MISSION OF FIGHTING HATE AND BIGOTRY. SPLC IS KNOWN FOR EXPOSING HATE GROUPS AND HAS WON SEVERAL CASES ACROSS THE COUNTRY AGAINST THESE GROUPS. IN 2009, THE SPLC IDENTIFIED MORE THAN 900 ACTIVE HATE GROUPS IN THE UNITED STATES.

videotape and televise it. I declined the offer, believing the Klan would not cooperate if news media people were sitting in the room. I wanted a genuine opportunity for growth and dialogue, and I didn't believe having an audience would allow that. We held the class at the Ramada Inn-Civic Center Hotel in Birmingham. I talked about the "oneness of the human family" and forgiveness and more. It lasted about three hours. Three of those who attended the class resigned from the Klan.

CHAPTER THIRTEEN

FREE AT LAST

We usually think of the movement as a vehicle for freeing Black folks, but it frees white people as well. A beautiful and moving example is seen in the story of my experience at a small burger place in Nashville, located in the area of Methodist headquarters, Vanderbilt University, and Scarritt College. My office was nearby in the Methodist Board of Discipleship building, so the restaurant was conveniently located. I usually encountered the same waitress, who repeatedly told me, "We don't serve Negroes." I would sometimes carry a sandwich, carefully wrapped in a napkin, and after the refusal, I would unfold the napkin and eat my sandwich right there. They didn't object, although I am sure they did not like it. Once when she said, "We don't serve Negroes," I responded, "I didn't order Negroes," or "I don't eat Negroes."

After a few weeks, the mayor met with business leaders and reached an agreement that they would desegregate several restaurants, including my burger place and Morrison's (now Piccadilly). I was out of the city, and my wife informed me over the telephone. I could not wait to return to Nashville to visit my burger place. When I entered the place, I could have sworn I saw my waitress smile. She proceeded to ask me, "May I help you?" I ordered a hamburger and a Coke. "How do you want your hamburger?" she said with a slight smile. I said, "Well done." When she served me, she stood for a moment and hesitatingly inquired, "May I pay for your hamburger?" I was shocked and unsure how to answer her. Finally, I said, "Okay, sure. But why do you want to pay for it?" Her eyes filled with tears as she explained, "You don't know how painful it has been for me to refuse you service. I'm a Christian woman, but I was under orders of the management, and there was nothing I could do. I need this job. I have three children to feed. My husband was killed in an automobile accident, and I am all they have." By then, her eyes were not the only ones filled with tears. I finished my hamburger and made a hasty exit.

The words of the waitress translated to "Free at last! Free at last! Thank God Almighty, I'm free at last!" Nothing ever showed more clearly how the removal of the shackles of segregation lifted a heavy weight from the shoulders of the people of faith, Black and white, both the oppressed and the oppressor.

In another instance the movement freed a man among the powerful elite. I was delivering a speech at Alabama State University in Montgomery when I was handed a message from the former governor of Alabama, George Wallace, who was now bedridden and could hardly speak audibly. He asked if I would come and pray for him. I agreed to do so. Following the prayer, the governor revealed the major reason he wanted me to come to his bedside. He said, "I understand you are a friend of Ted Turner, the media mogul. He's producing a movie on my life, and he portrays me as a womanizer and a heavy drinker. Neither of these is true. I'm not concerned about that, but he also in the film has a longtime employee and associate of mine, a Black man, plotting to kill me." Wallace was greatly disturbed by this. He always expressed fond admiration for the man and did not want the world to believe that the man hated him and wanted to kill him. "Nothing could be further from the truth," Wallace said. "I want you to ask him to affirm what I'm saying," he continued. The man was standing in the room as Wallace spoke. He urged the man to tell me that the story was false. I assured both of them that such a declaration was not necessary, for I did not believe for a minute that the servant wanted to kill his employer and friend. I recognized that if he had any desire to kill him, he had innumerable opportunities.

Earlier, in March of 1995, as I led the thirtieth anniversary reenactment of the Selma to Montgomery march, Wallace met us at St. Jude School, located on the edge of Montgomery. He apologized for his club-wielding troops in 1965 at the Edmund Pettus Bridge and generally for his vicious opposition to our goals and objectives. Later he declared his love and friendship for a Black man who worked for him for years and asked me to intervene with Ted Turner on the movie. He once again expressed sorrow for his behavior. On his death bed, his utterances could be translated to "Free at last! Free at last! Thank God Almighty, I'm free at last."

CHAPTER FOURTEEN

ELUCIDATE BEFORE YOU CELEBRATE: MAKE IT PLAIN

At this sixteenth year of the King holiday, it's time to assess and re-assess our understanding of this holiday, as well as the nature and appropriateness of our celebration. Since 1968, when Representative John Conyers introduced legislation to make Martin's birthday a national holiday, we find ourselves at a critical and pivotal point in the nation's history. Not only are we observing a new century (and millennium), we are witnessing the birth of a new era. The nation is in a transitional matrix; we are witnessing the redefining of a nation. There are forces seeking with titanic megabytes to redefine and remold this nation in their own image. We need a lucid understanding of the nature and purpose of the holiday, which can be a powerful means of assisting the nation to translate the ideals and values inherent in the holiday into public policy and personal perspective—blessing the redefinition.

Let's begin with a dose of elucidation, making it plain. Those of you who may remember Daddy King (Martin Luther King, Jr.'s father) will recall that one of his favorite admonitions to the preacher was "Make it plain." Thus, elucidation. The holiday honors the man, Martin Luther King, Jr., whose courage empowered him to challenge principalities and powers; whose intellect enabled him to wrestle with analysis without paralysis, to engage in intellectual calisthenics in both logical and syllogical dialectics; whose understanding of the historical energized him to illumine yesterday, clarify today, and envision the future—a man whose devotion to the pursuit of justice led him into the fiery furnace of political crossfire. He fought the good fight and inspired the least of these to embrace hope, exercise faith, and stand on the promises of God. The holiday honors the man: "You 'da Man, Martin." But elucidation won't let us stop there.

The holiday does more than honor the man. I believe Martin would be the first to agree with me. Beyond him, the holiday symbolizes the national commitment to racial justice and human dignity. By this holiday, the nation amplified its mission under God to sound a lucid call to freedom from every mountainside and from sea to shining sea. By this act, America stood at the altar of nationhood and repeated the vows to secure life, liberty, and the pursuit of happiness for all its citizens. We vow to love, honor, and obey. Love justice, honor truth, and obey the civil rights laws, in good times and in bad times, in sickness and in health. Not just till one political party or the other wins the White House, not just until the deficit is reduced nor the budget balanced, not just until your favorite team wins the Super Bowl, nor until the swallows come back to Capistrano, nor till there is a white Christmas, but till death do us part, till the saints go marching in, till the twelfth of never... and that's a long, long time! By this holiday, the nation declared before God and the community its intent to include the excluded and remedy inequities. By this holiday, the nation that once banished the red man, enslaved the black man, and relegated all who were not white to measures of political, economic, and social bondage comes on this day to renew those vows and promises this time to make good that promissory note that came back marked insufficient funds. This day must be a day of national conscience, a lucid call to find the lost chord and finish the unfinished task! But elucidation won't let us stop there.

Now commences celebration. The holiday provides the opportunity to redefine the nation in concert with the concept of the oneness of the human family: one in creation and one in the redemptive love of God; one in commonality of hopes and dreams for fulfillment. The celebration calls for the reordering of priorities. We must reject twisted values that have led us into dark alleys of materialism, balkanization, and terror. We have placed profit over principle, might over right, expediency over excellence; convenience cancels character, comfort steals conscience, and ends justify means. We have let fear drive us into armed camps, yet the more weapons we employ the more insecure we become. Our romance with guns has confused some of our children who seem to love guns more than

Ebony Magazine,
November 1993: "The 15
Greatest Black Preachers"

Lowery meets Nelson Mandela in
Johannesburg. Left to Right: Evelyn Lowery,
Nelson Mandela, Joseph Lowery, and Winnie
Mandela. Traveling to Southern Africa to attend
the Namibia Independence Celebration, SCLC
President Rev. Joseph Lowery also journeyed to
neighboring South Africa where he met with
ANC leader Nelson Mandela in ANC offices in
Johannesburg. Lowery also met with South
African white business leaders who wanted to
know the role white business community played
in desegregation of Southern U.S.A. In
Capetown, Lowery preached in Dutch Reformed
Church pastored by South African leader Allan
Boesak, and also met with mayors and
councilmen of several towns including Soweto,
many of whom were supporters of Chief
Buthelezi. Lowery urged white business leaders
in Capetown and Johannesburg to work
aggressively for black economic empowerment
and urgent unity between Inkatha and ANC
supporters. Lowery told the black leaders that
violence was self-defeating.

Crossing the Edmund Pettus Bridge commemorating Bloody Sunday. Left to Right: Jesse Jackson, C. T. Vivian, Joseph and Evelyn Lowery, and John Lewis.

March in Birmingham, Alabama, during a SCLC Convention. Left to Right: John Nettles, Evelyn and Joseph Lowery, Abraham Woods.

Joseph and Evelyn Lowery stand at memorial wall at the Southern Poverty Center in Montgomery, Alabama.

At March in Memphis 1968. Left to Right: Ralph Abernathy, Evelyn Lowery, Joseph Lowery, Chauncey Eskridge.

Morehouse College President Walter Massey joins the Lowerys as Ashby Street is renamed Joseph Lowery Blvd. in Atlanta, 2001.

Joseph Lowery and Fred Taylor being arrested protesting hazardous waste landfill in Afton, North Carolina, 1985.

Lowery receives Medal of Freedom, this country's highest civilian honor, from President Obama.

Medal of Freedom.

Delegation meets with Governor George Wallace following the Bloody Sunday March commemoration. Photo by Elaine Tomlin.

Left to Right: Cheryl Lowery-Osborne, Karen G. Lowery, Yvonne Lowery Kennedy, Rev. and Mrs. Joseph Lowery.

Lowery served as delegate to three United Methodist General Conferences in 1964, 1966, and 1968. In a historic session in 1966, he was elected to serve as presiding officer of the 1966 Annual Conference in Birmingham.

Lowery preaches at mass meeting. Pictures from the collection of Dr. Evelyn Gibson Lowery.

girls and in some instances, frightening as it may be, to love death more than life. We have glorified violence, sanctified war, maximized the material, minimized the spiritual, dehumanized the poor, trivialized social sensitivity, castrated compassion, ostracized the saints, and canonized the devil. We have affirmed violence as an acceptable means of resolving human problems by sending smart bombs on dumb missions and by remaining one of the very few nations that continues to say we are stopping killing by government setting the pattern for killing with the death penalty. To celebrate the oneness of the human family and to establish priorities based on spiritual and moral values is to commit ourselves to closing the economic gaps and remedying social inequities. Gaps were not created by osmosis, nor did they come into being by accident. Intentionality and deliberation came into play. If we are to close the gaps, we have to be intentional and deliberate.

Finally, we cannot bring a close to our elucidation without paying our respect to efforts to deal with globalization as we work from the perspective of Kingian theology. We must raise moral questions and unleash the powers of spiritual and moral force. We missed a glorious opportunity to demonstrate how to deal with the evil of terrorism. We must put an end to the widening of the cycle of destruction and death and violence. We must deal with the root causes of terrorism. Unilateralism and predatory preventive war may have squandered much of the world's support we enjoyed following 9/11. Have we lost our moral authority? Are we safer? Have we fertilized the breeding ground for terrorism? We must deal with the real weapons of mass destruction: poverty, greed, minimum wage, lack of health care. Jobs are not only fleeing to Latin America but now to India and China. I read the other day that 800 MRI analysts lost their jobs, where they each earned in excess of $100,000, and 200 people were hired in India at $20,000 each. Let's remember we serve a God who's got the whole world in his hands. He's a God of Atlanta and Afghanistan; Boston and Bagdad; Tallahassee and Tel Aviv.

I'm willing to trust God with the whole world. I still believe he's got the whole world in his hands. That's where our elucidation must begin leading up to our celebration.

FAVORITE THEMES

CHAPTER FIFTEEN

LIBERATION LIFESTYLES

If you hold to my teaching, you are really my disciples. Then you will
know the truth, and the truth will set you free.
—John 8:31-32, NIV

In 1984, we held eleven hearings in 11 cities on the crisis in health care. We learned from the health providers that about one-half or more of the factors that determine your well-being are related to your lifestyle! So, in 1985, I initiated a program called "liberation lifestyles"[1] to address these issues, embracing a lifestyle that makes you free at last—free from perverted values; free from deteriorating values; free from self-hatred; free from dependency on alien substances; free to respect ourselves; free to turn *to* each other and not *on* each other; and free to teach our dollars some sen$e.

Some have raised the question whether the major civil rights organizations that contributed so much toward advancing the cause of Black liberation in the past have had to change their traditional agendas in order to maintain their effectiveness as catalysts for nonviolent social change in the present and for the foreseeable future. Drugs, poverty, and violence are major crises that confront us. We must attack these problems as we remain vigilant to the problems of racism and exclusion. At the same time, we believe that much of our problem is that we are worshiping the material over the spiritual. That is why we are killing each other, and that is why people are expendable as long as the goal is money.

More than three million persons in the United States are homeless; one of three Black families lives in poverty; forty million Americans are poor, and most of them are not Black. We have painted poverty black and therefore made it easier to put on the back burner. Poverty is painful to everyone, regardless of color, caught in its devastating grip. People are dying in the ghettoes of despair and joblessness; people are dying in valleys of self-hatred and desperation. People are dying in suburbs of isolation and attempts to insulate themselves from inner-city suffering; dying while seeking escape from confused values up dead-end alleys. There is no conflict between criticizing the pursuit of the dollar and working for economic justice. We worked with Shoney's and secured a $90 million agreement. We need more commitment to joint venture programs with Black businesses and to a franchise program where Shoney's will help finance franchises as well as train people to work. Black organizations remain vital to our perspective, our sensitivity, our commitment, our love of ourselves, our turning to each other, our sense of worth, and our determination to chart our own future.

Afrocentric themes are designed to free us from myths and saturate us in truth about the homeland and our heritage and to empower us with authentic identity for our selfhood and indemnity from brainwashing, but we must never fall victim to the assault from without by our fault from within.

I was invited to Durban, South Africa, to speak at a dinner honoring retiring president Nelson Mandela. I also had the privilege of speaking on a panel with now new president Thabo Mbeki. Talk about manhood; talk about liberation. Twenty-seven years Mandela spent in prison but remained spiritually and intellectually free ... unbowed ... unbitter ... head high ... vision clear. This is the essence and quintessence of African manhood. I was invited because I represented the link between the anti-apartheid movement there and our freedom movement here. It was good to hear how our movement inspired them.

They are free politically, but they still struggle from the dregs of apartheid, from deadly violence, from disheartening poverty. As Mandela and Mbeki challenge them, the battle is in their hands.

When we talk about liberation lifestyles, we are talking about being healthy physically as well as economically, politically, and culturally. The battle is in our hands. Just as we declare when we wear Afrocentric clothes that we are taking on liberation ideas and attitudes, we must also embrace liberation lifestyles and declare that we will take charge of our destiny.

As we inspired South Africans to struggle to throw off the yoke of apartheid, would that we now could demonstrate how to cast off the yoke of letting others set our priorities. We are called to embrace lifestyles that make us free at last. We must take charge of our lives. We must stop whining about what we don't have and make better use of what we do have! If you can't keep up with the footmen, how are you going to run with the horses?

We are wearing a kente cloth *headpiece* with a *handkerchief head mentality*. The time has passed for just scratching and grinning and shuffling and saying "yassuh, boss." No, no.

The time has passed for our failure to get our priorities and values in order. It is time to stop majoring in minors: going for a giant car parked next to a midget house, wearing expensive shoes but walking in muck and mire of sloppy preparation for your children's education. Handkerchief head mentality means investing in drugs rather than books and the ballot.

Handkerchief head mentality means walking into traps set by the enemies and not being politically active. It means having Martin Luther King, Jr.'s picture on the mantel but not voting. Crackhead is synonymous with handkerchief head mentality; you cannot compete in the marketplace. The new Uncle Toms may not be scratching and shuffling, but they are shaking and breaking and stealing and taking from others. Handkerchief head mentality means men disrespecting women and making babies without making homes, and women letting men use them as bunny rabbit breeders. There are too many households with one income at minimum-wage level because you got minimum skills and minimum knowledge and you curse your children with a minimum future.

We must embrace liberation lifestyles, which view life as a sacred lease from the Creator. Liberation lifestyles will free us from self-destructive behavior; free us to turn *to* each other and not *on* each other; free us to support our institutions and to teach our dollars some sense.

Liberation lifestyles will put an end to deserting the good spouse of spirituality and having an affair with the prostitute of materialism and greed, producing offspring with the congenital defects of racism, sexism, abuse of sexuality, economic exploitation, suicide, homicide, and fratricide; experiencing a new birth of spirituality and strengthening of the family—both nuclear and extended. It is the village committed to raising children, meaning that we are interdependent; your child is my child, and my child is your child. Liberation lifestyles will challenge the nation to condemn economic violence with the same intensity we condemn street violence.

We must meet this crisis with a renewed sense of movement, with intensified efforts to restore values and provide jobs and job training, adequate health care and housing. We must embrace liberation lifestyles that make us free at last from confused priorities and crippling dependency on drugs; free to reach new levels of self-esteem; free to support our institutions and businesses; and free to work for public policies that lead to full employment and adequate wages.

Truth shall set you free. If you are my disciples, you will hold on to my teaching, though the winds of contemporary evil try to blow us away from our roots in dignity and your roots in faith. The Word says, hold on.

There is a God...free at last, great God Almighty, free at last.

NOTE

1. I introduced this theme at the 1985 SCLC Convention in Montgomery, Alabama. I have preached it with different foci over the years.

CHAPTER SIXTEEN

SINGING THE LORD'S SONG IN A STRANGE LAND

Sermon 1986 and preached in variations thereafter

How shall we sing the Lord's song in a strange land?
—Psalm 137:4, KJV

This song of the exiled, this lament, is soaked in sorrow, anchored in anguish, saturated with sadness, and not totally unlike what in another cultural context might be the blues! "The wail of a down-hearted frail." The Israelites were held captive in an alien land. The Old Testament is our book of passion. The children of Israel were uprooted but sought to hold on to their faith. Their bodies were in Babylon, the land of Saddam, but their hearts were in Zion. This land of paganism, barbarism, sought to crush their spirits, but they bravely sought to hold on. In their hearts they had a longing for Zion that their captors could not obliterate or obnubilate. (clef?)

Their saga in many ways parallels *our* own history. In our days of heavy oppression we too had a longing in our hearts for freedom, for liberation, that would not be crushed. We had a yearning and a burning that neither slavery nor the yoke of segregation could evaporate. No matter what the external, we found an internal that defied the infernal and fastened the eyes of our souls on the eternal. There was a fire in our bellies that slave masters couldn't drive out; dogs couldn't bite out; fire hoses couldn't wash out; billy clubs couldn't beat out; cattle prodders couldn't poke out; bombs couldn't blast out; guns couldn't shoot out; jails couldn't lock out; and money couldn't buy out.

While there are parallels to the Israelites' journey and *ours*, there are places where the trails separate. The Israelites cried, how can we sing the Lord's song in this strange land? We felt, how can we *not* sing the Lord's song in the time of trouble? There is, of course, a sense in which we must not be at home in an alien land, never at "ease in Zion." Yet there is another sense in which we must learn to live existentially in two worlds at the same time and sing the Lord's song. When the Israelites were asked to sing the Lord's song, they sat down by the rivers and wept. They hung their harps on the trees. We sang!

On Jordan's stormy banks I stand,
and cast a wishful eye
to Canaan's fair and happy land,
where my possessions lie.
I am bound for the promised land.
Oh, who will come and go with me?

I hear music in the air!

While I resist the agony of oppression, I claim the victory of being set free. We learned to cope with *what is* while striving to bring into being *what ought*!

Interesting, isn't it, that oppressors have appetites for amusement from those they oppress? In a small town in Alabama where I pastored, a white pastor dared to suggest that his church and mine join in an afternoon service around "Race Relations Day." It seemed like a good idea, but it turned sour. My choir was to sing, but I wasn't to preach. The proposed service was to be held in the other church, not mine. Strange land wherein a choir would entertain, but the message of the music was vetoed when a Black preacher couldn't preach in a *white* pulpit.

Our music in the church was not designed to entertain. While it is pleasing, to be sure, it is designed to declare our faith and praise God's faithfulness. To spread the good news. To keep the flame of hope burning. To proclaim that there is a balm in Gilead. Our music is old spirituals and new Gospel. We must be careful not to let the beat obscure the "meat"—the meat of faith and hope! I love the beat; just don't eject the meat. "I'm so glad trouble don't last always."

Now, to be sure, a strange land is more than geography. Any

situation or environment, any system that denies the sovereignty of God and the dignity of his children, *is a strange land*. Any condition that places the material above the spiritual *is a strange land*. Any society that bows down at the shrine of racial supremacy *is a strange land*. Any system of economics where less than 20 percent of the people own and control more than 80 percent of the wealth *is a strange land*. Anyplace where a handful have more than they will ever need, while more have less than they always need, *is a strange land*. Any practice that discriminates on the basis of race, color, gender, nationality, or sexual orientation *is a strange land*. Any society blessed with resources a-plenty and yet endures hunger, homelessness, and encyclical poverty in the midst of abundance *is a strange land*. Any culture that claims to love the Creator while devastating his creation is a confused culture and subsequently *a strange land*. Any civilization that chooses violence over nonviolence, war above peace, military rather than diplomatic solutions, is a mad, *strange land*. A social order wherein we have deserted the good spouse of spirituality and carry on an affair with the prostitute of materialism and greed, an incestuous affair producing offspring with congenital defects—racism, sexism, economic exploitation, drug addiction, gun addiction—*is a strange land*.

Likewise, singing the Lord's song is more than carrying a tune in the right key. Singing the Lord's song is doing the right thing. Singing the Lord's song is turning the other cheek when we know that an eye for an eye and a tooth for a tooth will leave us all blind and toothless. Singing the Lord's song is building on a faith that will not shrink though pressed by every foe.

Our cities and our nation have become in many ways strange lands. Our schools and our young people are living in strange lands, frightened by the meaningless in life. So many of our youth not only kill others but take their own lives. The church must sing the Lord's song: a message of hope, glory of life in the faith.

Singing the Lord's song in a new millennium means moving from *charity* to *love*. Newer Bible translations replace the word charity with love. Charity is expedient; love is essential. Charity is giving a hungry man a fish sandwich. Love is providing training opportunities so he can learn to fish. Love will make sure the water is not polluted so the fish will be edible. Love will make sure skills are developed to get a job. Love will create the ability to buy fishing equipment or the ability to go to the fish market. But love does not stop there. Singing the Lord's song is fighting for livable wages: minimum is strange land, and livable is Lord's song. Singing the Lord's song is making health insurance accessible and affordable.

Sometimes the church can become a strange land. Singing the Lord's song is being able to disagree without being disagreeable. Factions and cliques are strange lands in God's church. Romans talks about how we ought to love each other.

Sometimes home can become a strange land. The church must minister to families and strengthen them. Disintegration of families is a perilous land. Sometimes home can grow cold and strange. Restoring the strength of the family is singing the Lord's song in a strange land. Respecting your vows—focusing on doing whatever, whenever you can to keep your family together—is singing the Lord's song in a strange land. A wife went to church and heard the message to sing the Lord's song in her marriage. She decided she would let God sing through her life, and she found new life in the spirit. Her home was transformed into an oasis of trust and peace and love.

Sing us one of the songs of Zion. They hung harps on trees. We sang the Lord's song and found hope; even our blues had a flame of hope: "I may be blue, but I won't be blue always," and "The sun's going to shine in my back door someday." Our real source of hope was in songs of faith that not only gave us hope, but put us in the key of love.

"My hope is built on nothing less" and "weeping may endure for a night, but joy cometh in the morning"—these songs of faith assured us that everything would be all right. Hold on; help is on the way. Hold on, for we know how it will come out. God has already worked it out for us. "Blessed assurance, Jesus is mine!" Hold on.

A few years ago, I was anxious to see Arthur Ashe and Jimmy Connors meet in the 1975 Wimbledon singles championship.

Thankfully, God gave me a short sermon that day, and I rushed home to watch the match. Dinner is family time in our house, so I begged my wife to allow me to eat in the den because I needed to help Arthur beat Jimmy. "But, Joseph, you said we would eat at the table as a family every Sunday," Evelyn said. "I know, honey, we'll start next Sunday," I told her. I needed to help Arthur. Now, I know you presume it's because Arthur is black, and he would be the first Black man to win Wimbledon. Not so simple. I needed to help Arthur because he was older than Jimmy, and I thought this might be Arthur's last time to win at Wimbledon.

When I got in the den, my youngest daughter, Cheryl, and her best friends Lisa (Andy's daughter) and Blanche (Randy Blackwell's daughter) were laughing and keeping up their usual chatter. I told them, "Shut up! I'm trying to help Arthur." They continued their antics with no respect for my helping Arthur at all. "But, Daddy," she wailed. "Shut up," I told her. "Daddy, you said Sunday was family time," she said. "Don't confuse me with facts, girl. Be quiet. I'm trying to help Arthur," I told her again. He was struggling, and he needed my help. I have to admit I was perspiring and getting indigestion as I ate because I was so into the match.

These girls had no respect for my predicament. They were laughing and teasing me for being so stressed out. Finally, when I was shouting at the television and Arthur, and shouting again at them to "shut up," Cheryl looked at me and said, "Daddy, cool out. You're gonna have a heart attack. The match is already won. This is a rerun. Arthur Ashe won three sets to one."

Hold on! We already know how it comes out. God has already defeated your enemies. He gave his life on Calvary. Hold on to your faith. It's gonna work in your favor. God has already claimed the victory!

Sing the Lord's song in a strange land!

CHAPTER SEVENTEEN

BOYS TO MEN

When I was a child, I talked like a child, I thought like a child, I rea-
soned like a child. When I became a man, I put childish ways
behind me. —1 Corinthians 13:11, NIV

[David was about to die, and he called his son Solomon and told him,]
"I am about to go the way of all the earth....So be strong [my son],
show yourself a man, and observe what the LORD your God requires:
Walk in his ways." —1 Kings 2:2-3, NIV

We live in a tough age of unprecedented crisis in moral behavior. Our values have been perverted, our principles inverted, dishonesty inserted, good converted, and evil concerted. One of my friends told me he had stopped watching the news before bedtime because he couldn't sleep well since the reports were consumed with robbery, homicide, fratricide, infanticide, suicide, bodies found in car trunks, drugs and thugs, children having children, and children killing children.

The basis of all of this critical behavior is that man has substituted his will for God's will. We have engaged in the worship of things rather than the worship of God. In Exodus 20:3-6 (NLT) God says,

> You must not have any other god but me....You must not bow
> down to them or worship them, for I, the LORD your God, am a
> jealous God who will not tolerate your affection for any other
> gods. I lay the sins of the parents upon their children; the entire
> family is affected--even children in the third and fourth generations
> of those who reject me. But I lavish unfailing love for a thousand
> generations on those who love me and obey my commands.

This is an age in which we have let our moral principles sag. Poor people all around, and we don't even see them. This climate

73

of worship of things is not just in the Black community, but when the nation as a whole has a bad cold, we have pneumonia! In 1 Kings, David is trying to help us understand what it means to be a man. He said to his son, "Show yourself a man." Solomon already had most of the things we consider as part of manhood. He had the latest toga, he had the most recent version of a chariot, he had all the riches and jewels he needed, and he had youth. This culture worships youth. We dye our hair, lift our faces. Our community does not respect age like we ought to. We've forgotten that some of the greatest figures in history were elderly. Moses. Mandela. We need the wisdom of the old and the energy of the young to forge an unstoppable combination. I'm old, thank God. I considered the alternative: it's called dying young. I didn't care for it.

You know how you can tell if you're getting old, fellows? I came in the other night at two o'clock in the morning. My wife didn't even ask me where I'd been. I kicked the bed and said, "Wake up and ask me where I've been." George Bernard Shaw, a famous British playwright, said, "Youth is wasted on the young." When you're young enough to do it, you don't know how; when you're old enough to know how, you're too old to do it. Now, I don't know what you're thinking about. I'm talking about handling computers and stuff like that.

Solomon had riches, and he had youth. But David said, "Still, you've gotta show yourself a man." Not only that, but Solomon had power. He was going to be the king. Now, power can be good or evil. It depends on how you use it. We've got more power in our community than we use. That's what Paul was talking about when he said to Timothy, "Stir what you've got." But that's a different sermon.

In the Old Testament, one of the fellows said to the chief, "I wanna run with the horses." And the reply was, "I've been noticing you. You don't even keep up with the footmen." You want a Cadillac, but you're not doing anything with your Volkswagen. You want a million dollars, but you're not doing anything with the thousand I gave you. You're not tithing. I'm meddling now. Boys want to run with the horses, but they can't keep up with the footmen. Men understand that they don't deserve to run with the horses until they learn to keep up with the footmen, until they learn to do the little things, those things that we tend to overlook that are more important sometimes than the big things. I'm talking about moving from boys to men!

Black men have always resented being called boys because of the disrespect. I guess that's why we got into the habit of saying "man" all the time. We are always calling each other man: "Man this, and man that." But it takes more than declaring it to be a man. David helps us understand manhood by assuring us what manhood is not.

Some preachers and I had a meeting the other day with the mayor about the sales tax increase we are about to vote on. My finger is going to quiver as I vote for it because I'm voting to spend more money. But we've gotta do it because if we don't, our water bills will go up three times as much. We can't really blame the mayor. It's those folks way back there who chose not to tackle the problem. A fellow wrote a letter to the editor the other day and said we should name the sewers after our former mayors because the previous mayors did nothing about the crumbling infrastructure. We are reaping the sins of the fathers that are visited into the third and fourth generations. We can't blame this mayor. It's those folks way back there that wouldn't tackle the problem of the crumbling infrastructure, and we are reaping the sins of the fathers and mothers. I'm not leaving you out, mothers. You take credit for the good we men do, so take some credit for our shortcomings.

Let me mention a few things to consider as we transition from boys to men. We've got to examine our standards of excellence. We must distinguish between *heroes* and *celebrities*. We have a whole lot of celebrities, but we have few heroes. We have not taught our boys how to emulate heroes. The criteria for heroism are much stiffer than for celebrity. Boys can be celebrities. Mike Tyson is a celebrity. Academics are a better standard of excellence than athletics. We've got to teach our boys to embrace academics with the same vigor that they embrace athletics. There's nothing wrong with athletics. I'm a pretty good athlete myself, at least I used to be. I could swing a pretty mean 9 iron. The problem now is that my back won't keep up with my front. I love sports. But long after the ability to be an athlete has gone, you're gonna need your head. I say to boys, "If you think you can be like Mike, go for it. But for God's sake, have a plan B. Acquire some knowledge. Develop some skills." Manhood understands that we have to put a higher priority on academics than we do on athletics. We don't celebrate the honor roll like we do the touchdown or the dunk.

Take the NBA. Let's say there are thirty teams in the NBA. Let's say fifteen on a team. So that's four hundred fifty. That's all that will be in the NBA at a time. There are more boys on the corner up the street right now trying to be like Mike than in the NBA. So if you've got game like Mike, go for it. But for God's sake, while you're developing your muscles, develop your brain; develop your spirit. Move from boy to man.

We need standards of excellence. We must cherish service over entertainment; substance over style; content over excitement; helpfulness over hype; content of character over color of skin; quality of mind over speed of feet. The cheetah is the fastest in the jungle, but its speed doesn't help when the lion comes. It may be fast, but its speed does not equal endurance. When the cheetah gives out, the lion puts on its napkin for dinner. Slower but surer wins out. The lion doesn't have to run faster, just last longer than the cheetah to defeat it. What good are designer shoes if you're walking in the mud of vulgarity? Why should you be a national hero because you can beat up somebody? We have to care more about the content

GUION BLUFORD IS A FORMER NASA ASTRONAUT AND IN 1983 BECAME THE FIRST AFRICAN AMERICAN IN SPACE. DR. DAVID SATCHER WAS SWORN IN AS U.S. SURGEON GENERAL IN 1998 AND SIMULTANEOUSLY HELD THE TITLE OF ASSISTANT SECRETARY OF HEALTH. FROM 1993-98, HE WAS DIRECTOR OF THE CENTERS FOR DISEASE CONTROL AND PREVENTION.

of one's character than the impact of one's fists. Boys admire brawn; men adore brains. Too many boys know who Tyson is, but don't know who Bluford is. They know who Michael is, but don't know who Satcher is.

Young girls, don't get caught up in a trap. Would a young girl have gone to an honor student at Wiley or Morehouse or SMU had that promising young man invited her over at 2:00 a.m.? I believe you young ladies have a name for that kind of call. Young women, you have to move from girl to woman and know not go to any guy's hotel room at 2:00 a.m. You ought to have sense enough to know he is not inviting you to play Chinese checkers. But because he was a celebrity, she got up, put on her cute outfit, and went to the hotel. Even so, no matter what, fellows, if she says "stop" or "no" at any point, boys may not stop, but men say, "Oh, baby, but okay." And they *stop*. It's the woman's call. Manhood is not measured by how aggressive you can be, but how disciplined you can be.

We must choose spirituality over materialism. Boys get confused in their policies about weapons of mass destruction. Men will take their time and let the inspectors do their work to make sure before they send our boys and young women in harm's way. Men understand the real weapons of mass destruction are not over yonder, but they are right here. Forty-three million people in this country are without health insurance; that's a weapon of mass destruction. Millions of people live on minimum wage; that's a weapon of mass destruction. You may not like this one. We have half a million "Negroes" right here in Georgia not registered to vote; that's a weapon of mass self-destruction. Two-thirds of the people who are registered to vote don't get off their rumps and go to the polls on election day. Staying home from the polls is a weapon of mass self-destruction.

Back to academics: somebody whispered in the ears of Black boys that it wasn't cool to be smart in school. I don't know who told that lie. Somebody said that if you make the honor roll, there's something wrong with you. How stupid! I'll tell you what ain't cool. It ain't cool to be a fool and not prepare yourself to deal in a tough, competitive world. And then when you can't cut it, you wanna call me and cry that they discriminated against you. No, you discriminated against yourself when you were in school and didn't dig down and master your subjects. You've got the brain to do it. Think about that recent story about those kids who had this little drug scam. They tricked the police; they organized. If they put their brains to good use, they could master any subject.

The world needs to witness and appreciate the gentleness of manhood. Manhood is measured by the strength expressed in gentleness. The most powerful man who ever lived was also the most gentle. They nailed him to a cross, and he cried, "Father, forgive them."

At Central Church where I pastored for eighteen years, a family in the congregation lost the wife and mother to lupus. A devoted father lost his loving wife. A little girl lost her mother. As I sat in my study one Sunday morning before service, I saw the six-five, two-hundred-pound father walking his daughter to Sunday school. He kissed her good-bye, and she walked away. Then I saw him beckon her back. When she reached her father, he bent down and took his big, clumsy, fat fingers and rebraided one of her braids that was coming loose from her ponytail. I wept as I watched the love and care as he struggled to reach beyond his comfort zone and remove the yellow ribbon, take the unraveling braid loose, and rebraid it, strand by strand by strand, until he had perfected his daughter's ponytail. That was the strength and gentleness of a man.

We have to teach our dollars some sense. Our dollars are ignorant. They only know one way to go, and that's out of our community. We need to teach our dollars to go round and round in our community. We need to support Black-owned businesses and insist that those businesses that enjoy our support that are not minority-owned hire Black people in important positions and that they do business with minority businesses. That's teaching our dollars some sense.

Men must stand up for love. Love has dignity. The world needs the gentleness of manhood. We tend to think that manhood is measured in macho terms. But the greatest man who ever lived was a gentle man. When they nailed him to the cross; when they spat upon him; when they crowned him with a crown of thorns; when they put a whole rugged, heavy cross on his back; when they made him climb up Golgotha; this gentle man looked down upon his tormentors and said, "Father, Father, forgive them, for they know not what they do."

See, manhood is not measured in how much strength you have, but how you use your strength. Strength is best interpreted in gentleness. Authority is like money in the bank. The more you use, the less your balance. Real authority, moral authority, is knowing that it's there when you need it. But you never waste it; you never expend it on irrelevancies. You never shoot a cannon at a mouse. You save it for the elephant. I'm talking about gentleness.

What the world needs now is not more macho. What the world needs now is not more jet planes. What the world needs now is not more super engines. What the world needs now is not more smart bombs to send on dumb missions. What the world needs now is not more missiles to blow little children to hell and back and to terrorize their land for no reason. What the world needs now is the gentleness and the astuteness and the Christian spirit of manhood. We need boys to move to men.

Boys look for security in weapons. Men know the best weapon is in the whole armor of God. I'm talking about boys to men.

Boys are restless and impatient. They want to run before they can walk. Boys are energized by anything, but men know they must "wait on the Lord to renew their strength, to run and not be weary, to walk and not faint." I'm talking about boys to men.

Boys seek revenge; men know the Lord said, "Vengeance is mine." I'm talking about boys to men.

Boys flitter from bed to bed; men know that it may get you AIDS and you soon may be dead. I'm talking about boys to men.

Boys want to have their way in marriage; they wanna be "happy" and take their marbles and roam. Men respect the sanctity of marriage, concentrate mind, body, and soul on working on their marriages, and know it's cheaper to keep their wives. I'm talking about boys to men.

"Seek ye first the kingdom of God, and his righteousness; and all these things shall be added unto you." Move from boys to men.

CHAPTER EIGHTEEN

GOOD CRAZY: REMARKS AT THE COMMEMORATION OF BLOODY SUNDAY

Brown Chapel AME Church, Selma, Alabama, March 4, 2007

I didn't wanna speak before the senator[1], but you gotta take it when you can get it. I was supposed to preach at Tabernacle, but I got a headache. I told them I didn't wanna preach. I wanted to be here with the crazy folk.

Recently, I preached at a Catholic church in Chicago commemorating Martin's birthday. On that Sunday, as a Methodist preacher in a Catholic church, I prayed for a Muslim preacher. I prayed for Louis Farrakhan, who's in the hospital desperately ill.

Crazy things are happening. I looked out here in the audience, and there's the Muslim congressman clapping his hands to "Hold to God's Unchanging Hand." There are people in this country who say certain things can't happen, but who can tell? I got a physical a few years ago from my physician, and after the examination he said, "Your cholesterol is a little high." I thought I just needed to cut down on those peach cobblers and things like that. He said, "On the other hand, your good cholesterol is all right." I'm glad he reminded me that there's good cholesterol and there's bad cholesterol.

Like cholesterol, there's a good crazy and there's a bad crazy. You see, when Harriet Tubman was running up and down the Underground Railroad, she was as crazy as she could be, but it was a good crazy. When Paul preached to King Agrippa, the king said, "Paul, you're crazy!" But it was a good crazy. I'm saying we need more people in this country who are good crazy. You can't tell me what can happen when you have some good crazy folks going to the polls to vote.

God is not dead. He's the same God who stood by Shadrach, Meshach, and Abednego. Now, they were good crazy. They got in the fiery furnace, and Nebuchadnezzar looked and said, "How many did we put in the fiery furnace?" And somebody said, "Three." And Nebuchadnezzar said, "I see one, two, three, four. And the fourth one looks like the Son of God."

Now, I know you modern and sophisticated folk don't believe God gets in our business like that, but let me tell you what good crazy can do. The other day in New York, a man on the platform of the subway had a good crazy moment. He looked down between the tracks and saw a brother prostrate, doomed by the oncoming train, and he jumped down in the middle of the track and lay on top of him to protect him as the train passed over them. I asked a friend of mine to go out there and measure how deep it is, and the deepest measurement is twenty-six inches. Ain't no way in the world for one man to get on top of the other in twenty-six inches and the train go over them! But it happened. The only thing the train touched was his cap where it left a little grease. That was the same God! The same God who was with Shadrach, Meshach, and Abednego, that same God is here today.

Somethin' crazy may be happening in this country. Oh, Lord! There is something in the atmos-

BROWN CHAPEL AFRICAN METHODIST EPISCOPAL CHURCH IN SELMA, ALABAMA, IS CONSIDERED THE HEADQUARTERS FOR THE CIVIL RIGHTS MOVEMENT. THE HISTORIC CHURCH WAS WHERE THE SELMA TO MONTGOMERY MARCH BEGAN. ON MARCH 7, 1965, PROTESTERS GATHERED OUTSIDE BROWN CHAPEL TO BEGIN THE FAMOUS MARCH. AS MARCHERS APPROACHED THE EDMUND PETTUS BRIDGE, JUST A FEW BLOCKS FROM THE CHURCH, THEY WERE ATTACKED BY POLICE BRANDISHING TEAR GAS AND WEAPONS. THIS VIOLENT ASSAULT IS KNOWN AS BLOODY SUNDAY.

phere, and I believe we are on the cusp of something we've never seen before. Keep watching. Something good crazy just may happen in this country!

NOTE

1. The senator referred to is then-Senator Barack Obama.

CHAPTER NINETEEN

CHAPLAINS OF THE COMMON GOOD

To each is given the manifestation of the Spirit for the common good.
—1 Corinthians 12:7, ESV

REFLECTION

Nobody respects my retirement. When I retired from SCLC in January of 1998, a group of us formed the Coalition for the People's Agenda. Every Tuesday, we have a luncheon meeting with representatives of advocacy organizations including civil rights, peace, labor, environment, human rights, women's issues, justice, youth, in addition to concerned private citizens. We deal with issues related to improving the quality of governance. At the end of each meeting, we chant a line, which has become our theme: "We are Chaplains of the Common Good." Chaplains are spiritual leaders who are in many instances responsible for reading the scripture and prayers in community organizations. We see it as far deeper than that. We see a Chaplain as the conscience of the organization, constantly nudging us to do what is

THE COALITION FOR THE PEOPLES' AGENDA IS AN ATLANTA-BASED ORGANIZATION FOCUSING ON JUSTICE ADVOCACY. THE GROUP REGULARLY PRESENTS COMMUNITY EVENTS THAT HIGHLIGHT VOTER REGISTRATION, TOWN HALL MEETINGS, AND CANDIDATE FORUMS TO HELP CITIZENS BECOME INFORMED ABOUT ELECTIONS. THE ORGANIZATION WORKS WITH OTHER JUSTICE AND VOTER ADVOCACY GROUPS.

right. We see ourselves as "Chaplains of the Common Good." I have used this theme in many sermons.

****

Chaplains nudge us toward the common good. Through scriptures, prayers, and sometimes a clap of thunder, they jar us to righteous reality. Sometimes it's a flash of lightning making plain the landscape of societal ills; sometimes it's a whisper into our stilled conscience; sometimes it's an alarm clock saying it's time to rise; sometimes it's a bugle call to engagement; sometimes it's a cool breeze of thankfulness following the glory of triumph or agony of defeat; but it's always on the side of the Creator, always calling out the best in us for the common good.

We are in the season of Martin Luther King, Jr.'s birthday. Martin Luther King, Jr., was more comfortable serving than being served. His deep and radical commitment to the common good is indelibly stamped on history—giving rather than receiving. Indeed the Martin Luther King, Jr., holiday honors the man, scholar, preacher, prophet, teacher, crusader, healer, and disturber—a man whose courage empowered him to challenge principalities and powers; whose intellect enabled him to engage in logical and illogical dialectics; whose understanding of the historical equipped him to illumine the past, elucidate the present, and envision the future. He was a man whose pursuit of justice for the least of these led him into the fiery furnace of political combustion and fiscal frenetics, but like the militants of the Old Testament—Shadrach, Meshach, and Abednego—he found strength and deliverance in partnership with the Creator. He gave hope to the hopeless, power to the powerless.

It has been 40 years since the assassination of Martin Luther King, Jr. There is symbolism with 40; 40 is the age of responsibility; in athletics we have the 40 yard dash; 40 years wandering in the deserts; the flood was 40 days and 40 nights. We have lost much of the fire in our belly for the journey. There was a time when fire hoses couldn't wash it out; billy clubs couldn't beat it out; bombs couldn't blast it out; jails couldn't lock it out; and, thank God, money couldn't buy it out! It's time to renew and revive the call to serve the common good.

Incidentally, there is a grave danger that we are attempting to put King on some rotunda of sentimental irrelevancy—ennobling the messenger but ignoring the message, enshrining the missionary but incinerating the mission. As chaplains of the common good, we are called not only to honor the preacher but to heed the sermon and to put the salve of our vows on the affected areas of life in these United States. Martin's message and the meaning of the holiday lose their power when we don't apply the moral purposes to public policy and private practice.

We need to apply the principles and purposes set forth in the ministry of Martin Luther King, Jr., to matters of international relations. We need to put forth the message in no uncertain terms that there is no military solution to the crises in the Middle East. Even the highest military authorities have told us that war is not the answer.

We are called to apply the healing salve of Martin's message to the affected area of economic justice. We are plagued today by escalating poverty on one hand and a small group of rich folks getting richer on the other. There are growing disparities. Martin died in the midst of a struggle to improve the quality of life of sanitation workers in Memphis, the least of these—not in service but in income. There is no such thing as menial work—just menial pay. There is a growing disparity between those who have so much and those who have so little. A recent Swedish study compared the average income of CEOs and the average income of plant workers. What's fair? The study showed CEOs in Sweden earn five to seven times what workers earn. In the U. S. they earn 200-plus times as much. There's something wrong with a system wherein a handful of people have more than they ever need while masses have less than they always need. CEOs are fired and take home millions in severance while workers struggle to maintain pensions. Workers are laid off and wages reduced. The U. S. House of Representatives lifted the minimum wage the other day—a minimum increase, but at least moving in the right direction. Chaplains of the common good must call the nation to address the issue of the moral nature of poverty. Poverty is a moral issue.

We must apply the healing message of Martin to opportunities in education. Education holds the key to unlock the pathways out of the pits of poverty, yet poor people have the poorest schools. We continue to witness an assault on efforts to close the gaps and remedy inequities. Affirmative action is simply being as intentional about closing the gaps as we were about creating them in the first place.

You have five fingers on one hand, and if two are infected, you must make extraordinary efforts to minister to the infected fingers or the whole hand is imperiled. We must apply Martin's message to concepts of oneness of the human family. We are one in Creation—one in redemptive love and hopes and dreams for meaning and fulfillment. Martin said there is no path to fulfillment for whites that do not intersect paths to fulfillment for Blacks. We are inextricably bound together.

In the *Merchant of Venice,* there is a stirring comment on oneness. Does one not find joy or sadness in the same vagaries; too often we are divided by weapons of mass distraction. Demagogues seek to divide us with wedge issues that call for communication and negotiation, not hostility and polarization: abortion and same-sex relationships are issues about which good people can have honest disagreement, but these issues should not be used to turn us *on* each other rather than *to* each other. As we accept our common humanity, we can work it out in good will and with respect.

Chaplains of the common good are called to find the joy in struggling together for common goals. They celebrate the call for renewed energy. Luke's children of darkness seem better organized and more energized, but if we get fired up, we have access to fire from on high. We need to get fired up. We are not alone. The moral force of the universe is on our side. Remember the three Hebrew lads who were put in the fiery furnace? Nebuchadnezzar said, "I see four" and the fourth looked like the Son of God. Chaplains of the common good are not left alone.

The other day, I arrived in Kansas City around the fourth quarter of a national championship football game. To my surprise, I discovered that the underdog was leading, 30-14. This must be a mistake, I said. The mighty frontrunner had a Heisman trophy quarterback and had won nineteen straight games. What was overlooked was that the underdog team was fired up. The real game is not won on the computer, nor in the media, but on the field of battle.

CHAPTER TWENTY

HAM AND TURKEY SANDWICHES

In February 1982, we began a March to Washington in defense of Maggie Bozeman and Julia Wilder, two Black women, both former teachers, who were falsely accused of voter fraud in Pickens County, Alabama, and were sentenced to jail. The march, through five states, was also held to demand extension of the expiring section of the Voting Rights Act of 1965.

Beginning in Carrollton, Alabama, on a cold wintry day in February, we gathered on the courthouse steps. SCLC staff, community leaders, and other activists were headed for our next stop, a twelve-mile march to Aliceville, Alabama. Some community leaders were discouraged; they told us that the sheriff was going around in the community promising hams and turkeys in an attempt to prevent the march and discourage the community from meeting us at the rally when we arrived in Aliceville. We shook our heads in disbelief.

It started to rain—a cold rain—before the march really began, but we weren't going to let that or anything turn us

MAGGIE BOZEMAN AND JULIA WILDER WERE TWO CIVIL RIGHTS WORKERS CONVICTED BY AN ALL-WHITE JURY IN 1982 OF VOTER FRAUD. THE STATE OF ALABAMA CHARGED THEIR SOLICITATION OF 39 ABSENTEE VOTER BALLOTS FROM BLACK CITIZENS WAS UNAUTHORIZED. THE WOMEN WERE SENTENCED TO A TOTAL OF NINE YEARS IN PRISON, WHICH LED TO SEVERAL NATIONAL PROTESTS IN RESPONSE TO THE HARSH RULING. MAGGIE BOZEMAN AND JULIA WILDER SERVED ELEVEN MONTHS BEFORE A U.S. JUDGE RULED THEY HAD BEEN IMPROPERLY IMPRISONED AND WERE PAROLED.

around. So we proceeded with the march, heading for Aliceville. I remember telling Cottonreader, a veteran staffer, to instruct everyone to walk close together in order to stay warm. I decided not to share with Evelyn how disillusioned I was, and that I could not believe our people would accept hams and turkeys and be bribed against our fight for justice. Hams and turkeys? I just kept trying to shake it off, but the closer we got to Aliceville, I could not escape the thought of the community staying home, not supporting Julia and Maggie, all so they could receive a ham or a turkey.

Lord, help! I said to myself. *Are you testing me? Please, send me a message.*

Marching twelve miles in the dead of the winter was more than a challenge. We sang freedom songs and prayed all along the journey. We were "picking 'em up and putting 'em down" with hearts heavy and feet tired. Hams and turkeys?

We finally began to turn the last corner of the twelve miles and entered the city of Aliceville. Cold, tired, and weary, we kept our hearts on our mission. We were determined not to let those who might have sold their souls for hams and turkeys discourage us. I prayed to myself as we walked toward the community center. And then, there they were, hundreds of supporters with marching shoes, welcoming and greeting us—and with baskets full of ham and turkey sandwiches! Glory, hallelujah!

CHAPTER TWENTY-ONE

WHO WILL BELL THE CAT?

Mississippi Boulevard Christian Church, Memphis, Tennessee

This is the thirty-eighth anniversary since Martin was taken from us. I come to Memphis every year because we must not let America forget where the roads of violence and hate lead. They lead to death and destruction. Always good to be here with your pastor, Dr. Thomas. He's a thoughtful and capable leader.

Read 1 Kings, the twentieth chapter, when you get a chance.

It's a story out of the Middle East, and it depicts the continuous struggle, the conflict, the war in the Middle East. And in this particular context, Ben-hadad, the king of Syria, was about to attack Ahab and the people of Samaria. And Ben-hadad had a tremendous military machine for that day. Ahab had hardly anything. Ahab was a sorry king. Hello? He had a sorry wife. I'm not saying that's what made him a sorry king. I just said he had a sorry wife. Well, you ladies do have to take some responsibility because when we do well, you always say, behind every good man is a good woman. So, if he flunks, you need to take some of that responsibility.

But Ahab was exceedingly resourceless, and even before the battle began, when word reached Ahab that Ben-hadad was demanding things out of the coffers—riches, cattle, sheep, and even families, women, and children—he threw up his hands and gave up. But God planned otherwise, and God sent a prophet to speak to Ahab. The prophet said unto him that God did not want his people to be trampled and destroyed—devastated. And he gave Ahab a plan wherein he could resist and even overcome the terrible challenge of the Syrians under Ben-hadad. And Ahab took the plan, and he wrapped it around his brain and his spirit. He got happy, and he called his lieutenants together and said, "God has sent us a plan, and we're gonna work the plan, and we can overcome." And all of a sudden he thought a minute, and he said,

"Hey, go catch the prophet. I wanna ask him one question. It's a wonderful plan, but who is gonna lead the charge?" And the prophet said, "*You* are going to lead the charge. God has not put you in this place for your own personal aggrandizement." As Paul said in 1 Corinthians 12:7, God has made himself manifest unto us for the common good. We're not to use God's benefits and blessings for our own selfish agenda. They're for the common good. And so you must lead the battle.

Every time I think about that story, I think about another story in the fable world. You are probably too young to know this story, but when I was a boy, there was a story about a family of mice who were always devoured by the cat. They didn't ever get to be old mice. The cat would destroy them. One of the little mice hung out around Memphis State or LeMoyne-Owen College or somewhere like that and learned some strategies and skills and wisdom, and he came back to the elders and said, "Listen, I've got a plan for dealing with this cat. The problem we have is not that the cat's so fast; it's that the cat's so quiet. We can't hear him. Stealthy. Furtive. And before you know it, he's on us, and we can't get out of here. So, I've come up with a plan."

"What's your plan, young man?"

"My plan is to put a bell on the cat. And when the cat is coming, he will go ding-a-ling, and we can hear him, and we can get out of here."

The old mice said, "Doggone. Why didn't we think of that? We're glad you hung around Memphis State and LeMoyne and brought us this brilliant idea."

So the mice threw a party. Way over in the middle of the night, an old mouse stood up and said, "I don't mean to be a party pooper, but I do have one question. It's a great plan. But who will bell the cat?"

I come this morning in the context of that story to say that the soul of America is imperiled. I don't remember a time when the soul of America was so close to where that little fella who just sang said he would go if he didn't love the Lord: to hell. A man named Kevin Phillips, who is a Republican strategist, wrote a book *The Emerging Republican Majority*. He saw all this stuff coming. He

91

has a new book now, *American Theocracy,* a good book to read and study. He is credited with developing the Republican southern strategy, so he has some credibility. What he says is that as he looks at America today, the culmination of things, the recipe that we're using, the ingredients we're putting in the pot that constitute America today as you look to the future, he says her soul is in trouble. He foresees the decline and fall of the empire. See, don't ever get so secure that you don't think you can fall. The Roman Empire, France in our own time, the Dutch Republic—they all were mighty, but they fell. God doesn't love ugly for too long.

But Phillips says the things that are in the recipe that portend the fall of the empire, and one thing is big oil. I just read they are making billions not annually, but quarterly. Right out of my pocket. I'm gonna buy me a moped; better yet if I had somewhere to keep it, a mule. Big oil. And we've never had an administration so tied to big oil. Even "Condaleezy," Alabama sister, tipping across the stages of the world, carrying America's diplomatic strategy with her, even she has an oil tanker named after her. I don't know the background, but they say she's a millionaire. She's a brilliant girl. I don't know how her politics got so messed up. But anyway, big oil is one of the things Phillips cites as part of the recipe tearing at the soul of America.

The other thing is a growing disparity between those who have so little and those who have so much. A handful of people have more than they will ever need, while the masses of people have less than they always need. Something's wrong. Let me tell you another thing he mentions in the recipe: tax cuts for the rich. Hello? We've got the recipe, baby. Get your house in order. I don't know when it's gonna happen, but we keep on going.

Another thing he says that is in the recipe is the political right in power and the religious right hooked up with the political right, which ought to be called the political wrong and the religious wrong. They're just as wrong as they can be. Whoever heard of a Christian leader calling for the assassination of a head of a nation with whom we have disagreement? Whoever heard of religious people sanctioning war? How do they sing about the Prince of Peace?

But all of these things are in the recipe. We need the prophet to come and tell us God's plan. Who is going to bell the cat? Who's gonna deal with this tragic potential for America? Sandra Day O'Connor, the first woman on the Supreme Court, made a speech the other day, and she talked about the assault on the judiciary and how people like Tom DeLay and that bunch are trying to devastate and ravage the judiciary and, with the cooperation of the president, deposit upon that Court people who make Clarence Thomas look like a flaming liberal. She said—Sandra Day O'Connor, not Hillary, but Sandra Day O'Connor, a Republican conservative said—that kind of assault on the independence and integrity of the judiciary will lead to a dictatorship. I tell you, the soul of America is in trouble.

The last, most tragic study I want to mention is a study on young Black men. If the Memphis papers didn't carry it, ask them why. Young Black men are in trouble. *Seerus* trouble, not serious. There's a difference between serious and *seerus*. You see, serious is like a headache, and *seerus* is like a heart attack. Young Black men have no skills, no ambition. Hanging out on the corner. Afflicted with a couple of diseases; one of them is called ignoramusitis. Who's gonna bell this cat?

Now, listen, we must not stop fighting the system. The system is responsible for all this mess. But somewhere along the trail from back there to up here, somewhere, we must take responsibility for belling the cat. Now, make no mistake. I make no apology for demanding more from the government. The fact that the government does not do does not mean it ought not do. The government is sorry, but it's ours, and we need to make it right, so we've got to keep working. Too many Negroes are sitting around not voting and not participating in the political process. I tell ya right now. You had better be glad I'm not God. I would send every one of you who did not vote straight to hell. When I think of all the blood, all the sacrifices, and when I think about the future of young people, you're too slow to get involved. It's your future, not mine. My future is back yonder. Your future is out there. Get up, and bell the cat! Young people, if you wanna honor Martin's memory, get up, organize, mobilize, agonize, cogitate, agitate, and bell the damned cat!

Young Black men between the ages of eighteen and twenty-four, one out of four is in trouble with the system—either in jail, on probation, on parole, or about to go to jail. We have to look inside. I know the system; the system has put me in jail and shot at my wife's car. I know the system, and we have to keep fighting. But there are some things *we* must do for ourselves. And one of them is to stop letting our young Black men suffer from ignoramousidous and think they don't have to learn in school. Young Black men have to study and work hard, learn and get their brains in order. It's not enough to make our girls smart and let them go to college. We need to find ways to give awards to young Black boys who get good grades in school, who study, who apply themselves.

Ben Carson talks about how his nephew just studied all the time and the girls called him a nerd. The girls were interested in the athletes and the cool cats. We need to start building systems within our system to encourage and reward boys for their hard work and mental achievements. Look at those nerds, girls. You wouldn't look at them when they were studying. Now they've got a house on the hill and a Bentley in the garage. And those cool cats, you can't even find them.

The other disease we've got to work on with our boys is houndogitis. "He ain't nothing but a hound dog," sniffing around at some dog in heat. And we've got too many weak girls who heat up too easily. I tell the boys, let the girls be strong. Don't exploit them because some are fearful they won't get a man because of statistics. Let them be self-respecting because you're gonna marry one of them one day. And you don't want her, once you marry her, to conduct herself in such a manner that while you're at work. . . . Let her be strong. Admire her tenacity; admire her inner strength. That's the girl you want at home when you're at work. Girls, be strong. It's not as desperate as you think. Nine minutes of sweet talk, nine minutes of ecstasy, nine months of expectation, and a lifetime of deprivation. Bell the cat!

This is something we've got to do. The Chamber of Commerce isn't going to bell that cat for us. We must lead that charge. We must develop priorities that speak to our weaknesses and stop hiding behind the facts of what slavery did to us. I know what slavery did. Yes, it had its impact. But there's a power, there's a God who sent us a message: "You are my child. I made you in my image. If you're Black, it means I held you close to my bosom so long that you got scorched and darkened, and you're more like me."

God has sent us a plan; now work the plan. See, God is personal, but he's not private. God sent the prophet personally to Ahab, but then he involved the whole community. So we do what we can as individuals, and then we join arms with other people in the church, in the community, in the neighborhood, with organizations that are designed to bell the cat that nobody else is gonna bell but us.

Finally, we've got to enter into an era of discernment. That is sharp, critical, analytical thinking, and we've got to stop letting other people think for us. We even are letting other folk define us. If you don't know where you've come from, you won't know when someone's taking you back. If you don't know who you are, you may believe who your enemies say you are. I spoke with a fellow the other day, and he told me he took a group from his congregation to Montgomery last year to support that judge who wanted to put the Ten Commandants in the courthouse because he thinks God's Word ought to be in the courthouse. I said, "Man, please. Are you a fool? That judge, and judges all over the South, will sentence you without evidence, will hang you without due process, will cheat on you because you're Black, with the Ten Commandments hanging around their neck." I heard another preacher say the other day that we need to fight to put prayer back in schools, that the problem with schools is no prayer. I had prayer in school when I was a boy. It wasn't any better. We didn't have guns; we had fists. It's not prayer in the school; it's prayer in the home. That's what's missing: parents on their knees in prayer. How many of your children know how to pray on their knees in their bedrooms? How many children know that you know how to pray? How many children have you taught how to pray as you've taught them to ride a bike? Take your time, and teach them how to talk with God.

I come to the garden alone...
And he walks with me, and he talks with me,
and he tells me I am his own.

We've gotta learn to think. We're letting them hijack Jesus.
We've got to do something about the entertainment industry. We
are letting others stuff junk and trash and obscenity and vulgarity
down our children's throats. You don't have to have dirty music to
dance. I watched the Academy Awards the other day, and the best
song Hollywood could come up with for the whole year was something about pimps. And people went to jumping. What new level of
low life can we sink to that our music is all wrapped around pimps,
the scum of the earth? The other day a rapper in Atlanta—and I'm
not against rap because I don't know what they're saying—came up
with a contest to determine who has the prettiest booty. Fifteen- and
sixteen-year-old girls are going around getting their bootys ready to
exhibit in a contest. And their parents are all sitting around laughing, and saying, "Yeah, your booty is all right." Authentic beauty is
not in the booty. Authentic beauty is in the mind, in the spirit, in the
character. That's authentic beauty. Anytime you want to substitute
booty for beauty, you're gonna reap the whirlwind.

Your pastor mentioned Coretta's funeral. Let me tell you why
white folks are so upset. Three things. First, they don't want the
president exposed to an audience of independent thinkers; they
always screen and handpick the folk he talks to. But in Atlanta, he
was before an independent group of thinkers. And he heard the
truth. I could never have looked in the mirror again if God had
given me an opportunity to speak truth to power and I did not take
advantage of it. If you speak truth to power, and power is disturbed, what do you need to change, the truth or the power? One
of my friends told me I would not have done that in "our house."
In the first place, it wasn't my house; it was the Lord's house. I
wasn't called to preach the Gospel according to George W. I was
called to preach the Gospel of Matthew, Mark, Luke, and John.
The second thing is, they are culturally ignorant. Who made them
the authority on Black funerals? Where is their moral authority to
tell me what I can say at a Black funeral of a dear friend of mine's

wife, who was also my friend and colleague, whom I worked with and marched with and fought with on behalf of the least of these? Who do they think they are? What do they know about a Black funeral? Always in a Black funeral, we celebrate the life of the dead and challenge the living to take up the mantle and carry it on. That's what a Black funeral is about. The third thing is, they want to do with Coretta what they want to do to Martin: remove him from the movement. They want to put Martin in some rotunda of sentimental irrelevance. Always talking about "I have a dream." Look at the "Letter from Birmingham Jail" if you want to know who Martin Luther King was. Even Bush wasn't there because Coretta made good Girl Scout cookies. People were there because she advocated peace and justice and righteousness. That's why we were there. What was I supposed to talk about, wine and roses? They wanna put her over there with Betsy Ross and Mother Machree, but she belongs with Fannie Lou Hamer and Barbara Jordan and Shirley Chisholm, and that's where we've gotta keep her. And that's where we've gotta keep Martin.

Ben-hadad said, "We're gonna win the battle no matter what they do because their God is a God of the hills, and we're gonna fight in the plains. Therefore their God can't help them win." But oh, they didn't know our God. They didn't know our God. Yeah. He's the God of the hills, but he's also the God of the plains. He's the God of the high; he's the God of the low; he's the God of the midnight hour; he's the God of the early dawn's light; he's the God of the rich, but most of all he's the God of the poor; he's God when I'm down; he's God when I'm up; he's the God of Beale Street; he's the God of the silk stocking area; he's the God of the Baptists; he's the God of the Disciples of Christ. Oh, he's the God of all God's children. That's why we can win.

God is able if you're willing. He's able. He's able. Oh, my God is able. Oh, I wish I had a witness today. My God is able. Oh, yes, he is able. In the morning time, when I get sick, he's my doctor. When I'm in trouble, he comes and pleads my case. Oh, when I'm down, he lifts me up and takes my feet out of the miry clay. He puts a new song in my heart...oh, yeah. Who will bell the cat? *You* must bell the cat!

CHAPTER TWENTY-TWO

THE REDWOODS

Long before I thought about preaching, I remember seeing a picture in a magazine of a giant tree with a highway cut through its trunk and a van was driving through it. I was duly impressed by this giant tree, known as a Redwood. They are great trees. They can grow eighteen to twenty feet in diameter, over three hundred feet high, and they can live several hundred, even a thousand years old. They resist fungi and fire, and when the north wind meets a Redwood tree, it's apt to become the south wind. They are some "bad" trees.

I admire the Redwoods and have used them in illustrations as examples that humans might follow. One of the weaknesses of the Redwood is that its roots don't grow very deep or strong. To compensate for this, the roots grow in clusters and cling to each other, providing additional strength for the trees. It's said that for every foot in height they grow, the roots grow three times in width— connecting their roots, entwining with other Redwoods, creating a community, a family. They find strength in their interdependence. This is a marvelous advantage for the security of the Redwoods. Because of the intertwining, when you mess with the Redwoods, you're messing with the whole forest.

What a lesson for us! When the storms of life come, we are stronger when we depend on each other rather than on our individuality. What a fellowship, leaning on each other. We can live longer, grow stronger, taller, tougher if we turn *to* each other and not *on* each other. When you connect your future with my future, with the future of your neighbor and the future of the community, we have secured our future!

Blessed be the Redwoods.

WATCH NIGHT
SERMONS

CHAPTER TWENTY-THREE

WHAT YOU MEAN, HAPPY NEW YEAR?

God blesses those who... realize their need for him.
—Matthew 5:3, NLT

Life is a major in God and a minor in me.
I am a minor who may become major in God.
God and me are a majority.

At the end of one year and the beginning of the next, we engage in analyzing whether we are happy. We even seek to define and refine resolutions, all to see the status of our happy thermometer. Unfortunately the more we see, the unhappier we be. Theodore Roethke, the poet, wrote, "Self-contemplation is a curse / That makes an old confusion worse." Are we happier because we analyze what's wrong with us and our relationships? A group of psychologists asked two groups of people to do the same exercise about relationships. Only one group was to study and analyze the good and bad in their relationships while the other group was simply to give their gut feelings about their relationships. Those couples who did the analysis broke up within the next few weeks at a rate of 90 percent. The other group who used their gut feelings grew closer together.

Martin used to talk about "the paralysis of analysis." God knows we have studied race

WATCH NIGHT SERVICES ARE A COMMON YEAR-END PRACTICE IN MANY AFRICAN AMERICAN CHURCHES. THE TRADITION DATES BACK TO SLAVES AWAITING THE NEWS OF THE SIGNING OF THE EMANCIPATION PROCLAMATION, WHICH SECURED THEIR FREEDOM ON JANUARY 1, 1863.

over and over. The more we analyze, the more we polarize. So our text shouts that happy is being blessed by God. Listen, God blesses those who realize their need for him. Theirs is the kingdom of God. Writers seek to interpret or make plain God's loving care for the least of these: those who are poor in spirit; those who are usually rendered that way by oppression or by insidious insensitivity on the part of individuals and flawed public policy. The Bible always identifies God as concerned for the excluded, the downtrodden, and the bypassed. The New Living Translation indeed makes it plain. God blesses those who realize—not analyze—their need for him. It is our understanding of God's call and the need to respond that initiates our relationship with God. God seeks to reveal himself to us in so many ways, for he knows that until we see ourselves as his, we shall not find meaning in life, be blessed, and be happy. Until our lives are opened to his being and his will.

So, what do you mean, *Happy New Year*? If you mean you know and I must know that we are standing in need of an awareness of God and a relationship with him, then we do not need to analyze but realize and do it! Lord, I want to be a Christian in my heart, so that my gut feeling cries out, I need thee. Bless me now, my Savior. I come to thee. So my constant rehearsing of your presence in prayer, in worship, in song, in praise, brings into being in my heart, in my gut, my longing for you. When he calls me, I will answer. I have opened my life, my mind, my attitude, and my will. So no need to get bogged down in paralysis of analysis; just do it!

Praise has not benefited God as it has benefited men. Praise must translate into service. Authentic thanksgiving is thanksliving! I just want to praise him must mean I just want to serve him. I just want to love my neighbor. I just want to witness for truth. I just want to honor my commitments to my family. Is that what you mean when you say, *Happy New Year*? Then come on! Be ye doers of the Word, not just hearers.

Don't bog me down with trivia or irrelevancies. We find meaning and true joy and happiness in translating faith into works. *Happy New Year*! In a torn-down world, *Happy New Year* is waging peace—working to beat tanks into tractors, swords into plowshares, missiles into morsels of bread. Celebrate the Prince of Peace who calls us to study war no more. Is that what you mean by *Happy New Year?* Come on! Let's feed the hungry, clothe the naked, and house the homeless. *Happy New Year* is teaching our young that the wages of sin, drugs, sexual irresponsibility, and violence *is death*. Blessed is denouncing an entertainment industry that glorifies so-called music that degrades our women, makes violence attractive, gives so-called entertainers with minimum talent maximum exposure to make money and wreak havoc on our youth culture. Is that what you mean, *Happy New Year?* If you mean getting rid of trigger-happy law enforcement officers who shoot first and think later, *come on!* Happy New Year!

If you mean fighting greedy corporations and corrupt governments that find people victims of tsunami and hurricane, finding their land seized in New Orleans and Asia, come on!, *Happy New Year!* If you mean leaving my old hatreds and desire for vengeance in the old year, and grasping forgiveness in the new year, come on! *Happy New Year!*

If you mean a renewed awareness that I need Jesus in my life more than ever, come on! *Happy New Year!* If you mean I need to remember that it was

at the Cross where I first saw the light,
And the burden of my heart rolled away.
It was there by faith I received my sight,
And now I am happy all the day!

"Oh, happy day, when Jesus washed my sins away!" If that's what you mean, *come on!*
Happy New Year!

CHAPTER TWENTY-FOUR

WHAT WE WATCHING FOR?

Watch, therefore, for you do not know on what day your Lord is coming.
—Matthew 24:42, RSV

*Be on guard. Stand firm in the faith. Be courageous. Be strong.
And do everything with love.* —1 Corinthians 16:13-14, NLT

*I press on to reach the end of the race and receive the heavenly prize
for which God, through Christ Jesus, is calling us.*
— Philippians 3:14, NLT

In many places in the Word, we are admonished to watch and to pray. Many of these referred to the coming of the Lord, but not all. Many called us to watch, be aware, and I would add the word *discern* in regard to the coming, even before the physical. I believe the Lord comes to us in many ways, many times. He comes as a stranger. Jesus came as the least of these.

Watch Night services are a part of the Black church's rich history. We come together in faith to bring in a new year, grateful to have survived the last year, trusting God to bring us through the new year.

In reading about Watch Night, also known as Freedom's Eve, I came across John Hope Franklin's "The Emancipation Proclamation: An Act of Justice." It shares how meetings were held in D.C. in anticipation of the signing. (In D.C., slaves were actually freed by Congress in April of 1862, but all awaited the freeing of those in Confederate states and joined in on the New Year's festivities celebrating the signing.) There are also accounts elsewhere of slaves in the South meeting in homes and churches, singing and praying, awaiting word that Lincoln had signed the proclamation. They wanted to watch and pray. They were watching and praying clearly for freedom.

What we watching for?

Blessings? Yes. Forgiveness? Yes. But I want you to deal with the words you know but may not utilize often enough: *discernment, distinguishing, understanding right and wrong. Blessings:* We should understand the word in biblical terms, not a shallow definition—understanding in depth that we receive by giving. Selfishness and self-centered priorities are not sowing the seeds for a blessing. Authentic joy comes from giving. We are called to *be* a blessing, not just *get* a blessing.

What we watching for?

Forgiveness: Discernment reveals that it is in forgiving that we are forgiven. The Lord's Prayer challenges us to forgive as we are forgiven. Do all that you do in love.

What we watching for?

Weapons of mass deception: We watched around the world the execution of Saddam Hussein. An evil man, but what do we accomplish by killing him as he killed others?

What we watching for?

Discernment: Some Black folk embrace the death penalty.

As a nation, we should see we are in bed with those we want to save. Few nations still use the death penalty; even lethal injection causes butchering to kill. I have urged the city of Atlanta and DeKalb County to establish citizens' review boards to deal with this issue. In regard to Mrs. Johnson, the ninety-two-year-old lady here in Atlanta who was killed by the police force that should have been protecting her, an informant claimed to have purchased drugs from Mrs. Kathryn Johnson's home. The APD used a no-knock warrant, which allowed them to kick in her door. Frightened, she reached for her gun and fired a shot. The officers shot and killed her. Finding no drugs in her home, the officers later confessed to planting drugs from a different raid. The officers have been indicted, convicted, and imprisoned. Mrs. Johnson's family has been awarded a sizable financial monetary judgment.

I wish Mrs. Johnson had not owned a gun. *Discernment* reveals that guns are bad news that bring sad blues.

What we watching for?

An opportunity to bring an end to violence?

Acting for an Opportunity to Sow Seeds of Love

What the world needs now is love, sweet love. Respect. Kindness. There's too much meanness. There are so many examples of meanness: to remove former Congresswoman McKinney's name from the highway. The voter ID bill that basically serves as a poll tax. Both the Voting Rights Act and court rulings have said there can be no cost imposed for the right to vote. A stupid law was enforced, and the young man Genarlow Wilson is in prison because he had consensual sex with another underaged child. Politicians compete to see who can be the meanest.

What we must be watching for are opportunities to demonstrate what Christians mean about love.

Finally, *what we watching for?* Ways to strengthen family principles and ideals of justice and morality that must be taught in the home.

Our children need to see adults as instruments of love and safety and security. Every adult must share love, faith, decency, and compassion with children. If you don't have children of your own, volunteer with an agency, find some child who needs your love and example of stewardship. Children need to hear somebody pray, see somebody love, feel somebody care.

Again, when researching Watch Night, I found accounts where slaves gathered in homes and churches on New Year's Eve because slave masters and plantation owners established that the first day of the year was an accounting day. They would sell and buy property, including slaves, on New Year's Day. Can you imagine waiting and watching to find out if you would ever see your family again? Bound together by faith through trials and tribulations—family. But this may be the last time we see each other. *What we watching for?*

Until I went to Alexander City in Tallapoosa County, Alabama, in 1949 to pastor Haven Methodist Church, I had never heard the song that Sister Catherine Greer used to lead. I love this song and like to drum up the verses:

This may be the last time,
This may be the last time, children,
This may be the last time,
May be the last time, I don't know.

May be the last time I see your face.
May be the last time, I don't know.

May be the last time I call your name.
May be the last time, I don't know.

This may be the last time,
This may be the last time, children,
This may be the last time,
May be the last time, I don't know.

May be the last time we sing and shout.
May be the last time, I don't know.

May be the last time what you watching for?
May be the last time, I don't know.

This may be the last time,
This may be the last time, children,
This may be the last time,
May be the last time, I don't know.

What we watching for?

FAREWELL, MY SISTERS

CHAPTER TWENTY-FIVE

ROSA PARKS MEMORIAL SERVICE: FROM CEREMONY TO SACRAMENT

Greater Grace Temple, Detroit, Michigan, November 2, 2005

Eyes have not seen and ears have not heard how humility and greatness merged with such grace.

Twenty-some years ago, Mrs. Parks gave our youngest daughter, Cheryl, a wedding present—a check for twenty-five dollars. And then we didn't see her again for nine or ten months. Somewhere, my daughter heard me describing Mrs. Parks as a gentle giant. And then Cheryl came to me and said, "Daddy, today Mrs. Parks wasn't so gentle." I asked, "What did she do?" Cheryl said, "She asked me, 'Young lady, why haven't you cashed that twenty-five-dollar check? I can't balance my checkbook.'" She didn't understand that that check had become sacrosanct. And my daughter told her, "Mrs. Parks, I ain't never gonna cash that check!"

How do you honor a woman of this magnitude in a manner that is spiritually and historically correct? Ceremony is one way. This is the third ceremony I've been to—one in Atlanta, and I went to the one in Montgomery. Of course, I was there when Rosa Parks started, and I wanted to be there when she departed. And I'm here in Detroit today. Ceremony is one way you do it. Ceremony is a fitting tribute; it's translating thoughts into words and symbolic acts. But the truth of the matter is that ceremonies end with the benediction. You can't do justice to Rosa Parks letting your tribute end in ceremony. You have to move from ceremony to sacrament. Sacrament takes up where ceremony leaves off.

You see, ceremony is like putting a ring on her finger at the wedding. But sacrament is ringing her life with love and joy every day and every hour. Baptism is a ceremony, but living holy after the baptism is sacramental. And I believe if we are to do justice to Sister Parks, we must not stop with ceremony. The president of these United States engaged in ceremony in the Rotunda, but he stopped short of sacrament when he missed an opportunity to name somebody to the Supreme Court with the spirit of Rosa Parks for diversity and minority rights.

I call upon you today; let's don't stop with this ceremony. You must move from ceremony to sacrament. Sacrament ought to mean that never again can you let an election pass without getting up and casting your vote. Sacrament means that we must not tolerate homelessness or hunger in the midst of our communities. Sacrament means that we know where the weapons of mass destruction are. They're not in Iraq. They're in Detroit, Chicago, Atlanta, and Montgomery! That's where our weapons of mass destruction are. Fifty million people in this country with no health insurance—that's a weapon of mass destruction. Minimum wage is a weapon of mass destruction. In the spirit of Rosa Parks, we must sacramentally understand that drug addiction and drug selling are weapons of mass *self*-destruction. And in the spirit of Rosa Parks, we must rise up and sacramentally shed that addiction. Finally, we must understand the spirit of Rosa Parks in the spirit of saintly womanhood. We much teach our young people and children to stop having children. That's another weapon of mass self-destruction. I'm calling you to go from ceremony to sacrament.

In Montgomery the other day, as I spoke, was Dr. Condoleezza Rice—the Secretary of State, my ol' homegirl from Alabama. I took advantage of the moment. She couldn't move, so she had to sit there and hear what I had to say. Condoleezza made a beautiful tribute

> AFTER HER 1955 ARREST IN MONTGOMERY, ROSA PARKS AND HER HUSBAND, RAYMOND, WERE HARASSED AND EVENTUALLY LOST THEIR JOBS. AFTER RELOCATING TO DETROIT IN 1957, ROSA PARKS CONTINTUED TO FIGHT FOR EQUALITY FOR ALL PEOPLE.

to Mrs. Parks. But I said, "Dr. Rice, Sister Secretary of State, what a glorious tribute it would be if you and the governor of Alabama and the mayor of Montgomery would join John Conyers, Carolyn Kilpatrick, and John Lewis in extending the Voting Rights Act." That would be a sacramental tribute to Rosa Parks. She nodded her head and said she would.

Thank God for Rosa Parks! Now, let's move from ceremony to sacrament!

CHAPTER TWENTY-SIX

WHAT A FAMILY REUNION!
HOME-GOING CELEBRATION OF
CORETTA SCOTT KING

New Birth Missionary Baptist Church, Atlanta, Georgia
February 7, 2006

L ord, have mercy. How marvelous that presidents and gover-nors come to mourn and praise. But in the morning, will words become deeds that meet needs?

Sister Coretta was the First Lady of SCLC.

What a family reunion!

Rosa and Martin were reminiscing. They'd just begun to talk. When Martin seemed not to listen, he started to walk. The wind had whispered in his ear, "I believe somebody is almost here!" "Excuse me, Rosa," Martin said as he did depart. His soul was on fire. He just couldn't wait. His spirit leaped with joy as he moved toward the pearly gates. Glory, glory, hallelujah! And after forty years—almost forty years—together at last, together at last. Thank God Almighty, together at last!

Thank you, Coretta. Didn't she carry her grief with dignity; her growing influence with humility? She secured his seed, nurtured his nobility; she declared humanity's worth and vetted his and her vision of peace in all the earth. She opposed discrimination based on race. She frowned on homophobia, and gender bias was rejected on its face. She summoned the nations to study war no more. She embraced the oneness of the human family from shore to shore. She extended Martin's message against poverty, racism, and war. She deplored the terror inflicted by our smart bombs on missions way afar. We know now there were no weapons of mass destruction over there. But Coretta knew and we know that there are weapons of misdirection right down here. Millions without health insurance; poverty abounds. For war millions more, but no more for the poor. Well, Coretta had harsh critics. Some no one could please, but she paid them no mind. She kept speaking for the least of these.

As we get old, or so I'm told, we listen in to heaven like the prophets of old. I heard Martin and Coretta say, "Do me a favor, Joe. Those four little children I spoke of in sixty-three, they're fine adults now, as all can see. They already know, but tell them again. We loved them so dearly. Assure them we'll always be near their troubles to bless and sanctify to them their deepest distress. Tell them we believe in them as we know you do. We know their faith in God and their love for each other will see them through. Assure them that at the end of the tunnel awaits God's light, and we are confident they will always strive for the right. Tell them don't forget to remember that we're as near as their prayer and never afar. And we can rest in peace because they know who and whose they are."

What a family reunion! Lord, just the other day I thought I heard you say, "Coretta, my child, come on home. You've earned your rest. Your body is weary. You've done your best." Her witness and character, always strong. Her spirit, a melody from heaven's song. Her beauty, warm like the rays of the sun. Good night, my sister. Well done, well done.

THE FORTY-FOURTH PRESIDENT OF
THESE UNITED STATES

CHAPTER TWENTY-SEVEN

GOD MOVES IN A MYSTERIOUS WAY, HIS WONDERS TO PERFORM

REFLECTIONS ON THE INAUGURATION

Not long after the 2008 presidential election, I received a message on my cell phone from the president-elect. I returned the call, and when he answered, I said, "I'd like to speak to the man who will be the forty-fourth president of the United States." He said, "I believe that would be me, Brother Lowery." He told me he called to see if I would give the invocation or benediction at the Inauguration. I paused, then asked him to let me check my schedule. After a half-second pause, I told the president-elect I believed I could work it in. (Smile.)

A few days later it appeared in the paper that I would be doing the benediction. I started getting calls from friends telling me that they would rather I do the invocation. I told them to leave Mr. Obama alone; he knew how to run an inauguration. I had to explain to them that when I did the benediction, I'd have the last word!

So many people told me that when I'd stand on the Capitol steepway January 20, 2009, and look down the mall, I could view both the Washington Monument and the Lincoln Memorial. Mine eyes were too dimmed to reach the memorial, though they did discern the monument. Never mind, the eyes of my soul saw them both, and the ears of my recollection heard the voice of a thirty-four-year-old preacher summon a nation to rise from the valley of race and color to the mountaintop of "content of character." And there I stood, though cold and trembling, not only living to see that day, but matriculating in the curriculum! A ceremony that was part and parcel of the nation's 2009 response to the summons delivered in 1963! No way you could have convinced me in March 1965 as I delivered the "demands" of the Selma to

Montgomery march for voting rights to Alabama Governor George Wallace, that in January 2009, I would deliver the closing prayer at the inauguration of the forty-fourth president of these United States. God moves in a mysterious way!

Every citizen in the nation ought to be experiencing a metamorphosis, an epiphany, a regeneration! There's no way I can ever be the same. I have never liked the song we have chosen for our national anthem: "The Star-Spangled Banner"! I usually cringe when I hear it with its bombs bursting and rockets glaring. We should do better (like "O Beautiful for Spacious Skies"), but I confess that when the band played it following my prayer at the Inauguration, it was never so melodious. In spite of its militaristic nature, it was more tolerable and even for that one time beautiful! The song, of course, was the same, but I had changed! My country had changed! I had a new level of respect. We had climbed out of the pits of race and clan and onto the hillsides of hope and character and competence. It is not the end of where we ought not to be, or the end of where we ought to be, but it should be the "joy of a new beginning" of where we ought to be going! Every American should at least be as joyful as people in other nations seem to be. And it ought to be reflected in our behavior. In our attitudes. We should be thankful that a majority of voters did not yield to the temptation to be ruled by race and color rather than character and content.

No, we are not postracial, as the Harvard police–professor fiasco clearly reminds us. But we should relate to each other with a postinauguration attitude: new levels of respect and appreciation, a new spirit of thanksgiving for a God who moves in a mysterious way, his wonders to perform.

Particularly in the arena of law enforcement where the historicity is horrific should we relate to each other with cognizance of the history and awareness of the need for a new future.

In such a scenario, the officer would have said, "Excuse me, sir, but we had a call about a possible break-in here and we are checking it out. May I please see some identification?"

Professor: "Well, there is no break-in, and here is my identification. And as you see, I live here and teach at the university."

Officer: "Very well. We want to be sure that everything is okay. Have a good day!"
Professor: "Thank you! And you have a good day too."
President: No comment.
Radio clowns: No comment.
American people: Let's move on to health care reform and economic recovery and the joy of a new beginning!

God moves in a mysterious way,
his wonders to perform:
he plants his footsteps in the sea
And rides upon the storm.

THE INAUGURAL BENEDICTION
The Capitol Building, Washington, D.C., January 20, 2009

God of our weary years, God of our silent tears, thou who has brought us thus far along the way, thou who has by thy might led us into the light, keep us forever in the path, we pray, lest our feet stray from the places, our God, where we met thee, lest our hearts, drunk with the wine of the world, we forget thee. Shadowed beneath thy hand may we forever stand—true to thee, O God, and true to our native land. ("Lift Every Voice and Sing"—Negro National Hymn)

We truly give thanks for the glorious experience we've shared this day. We pray now, O Lord, for your blessing upon thy servant, Barack Obama, the forty-fourth president of these United States, his family, and his administration. He has come to this high office at a low moment in the national and, indeed, the global fiscal climate. But because we know you've got the whole world in your hands, we pray for not only our nation, but for the community of nations. Our faith does not shrink, though pressed by the flood of mortal ills.

For we know that, Lord, you're able and you're willing to work through faithful leadership to restore stability, mend our brokenness, heal our wounds, and deliver us from the exploitation of the poor, the least of these, and from favoritism toward the rich, the elite of these.

We thank you for the empowering of thy servant, our forty-fourth president, to inspire our nation to believe that, yes, we can work together to achieve a more perfect union. And while we have sown the seeds of greed—the wind of greed and corruption, and even as we reap the whirlwind of social and economic disruption—we seek forgiveness and we come in a spirit of unity and solidarity to commit our support to our president by our willingness to make sacrifices, to respect your creation, to turn *to* each other and not *on* each other.

And now, Lord, in the complex arena of human relations, help us to make choices on the side of love, not hate; on the side of inclusion, not exclusion; tolerance, not intolerance.

And as we leave this mountaintop, help us to hold on to the spirit of fellowship and the oneness of our family. Let us take that power back to our homes, our workplaces, our churches, our temples, our mosques, or wherever we seek your will.

Bless President Barack, First Lady Michelle. Look over our little angelic ones, Sasha and Malia.

We go now to walk together, children, pledging that we won't get weary in the difficult days ahead. We know you will not leave us alone, with your hands of power and your heart of love.

Help us then, Lord, to work for that day when nation shall not lift up sword against nation, when tanks will be beaten into tractors, when every man and every woman shall sit under his or her own vine and fig tree, and none shall be afraid; when justice will roll down like waters and righteousness as a mighty stream.

Lord, in the memory of all the saints who from their labors rest, and in the joy of a new beginning, we ask you to help us work for that day when black will not be asked to get back; when brown can stick around; when yellow will be mellow; when the red man can get ahead, man; and when white will embrace what is right.

Let all those who do justice and love mercy say, Amen.

THE JOY OF A NEW BEGINNING

Here at the finish line, we are called to a new beginning. I tell you gladly that in spite of trying times, we find joy in the reality of the mighty God we serve! We are in sainted company when we bask in the light that breaks through the darkness from time to time. The light broke through in 1965 when at the close of the voting rights march from Selma to Montgomery, Dr. King asked me to lead a group to deliver the "demands" of the march to Alabama governor George Wallace. The right to vote was now on the national agenda. The president of these United States (LBJ) soon signed the Voting Rights Act and went on national television pronouncing the words of the anthem: "We Shall Overcome."

We shouted for joy at this new beginning even while knowing that it was the joy of a new beginning and the challenge of a new chapter of the struggle. As we rejoiced at the promise of the vote and election to public office, we dared not even think of electing an African American president in our lifetime. Someday, yes, but now, no, not now! But what a mighty God we serve! I mentioned earlier that someone told me that when I stood on the steepway of the Capitol, I would be able to see both the Lincoln Memorial and the Washington Monument. I almost did, but there was a haze that day (plus I was using eighty-eight-year-old eyes). I did not only see those marvelous historic sites, but I heard the voice of a young preacher—forty-six years earlier—standing on the steps of the Lincoln Memorial, issuing a summons to our nation to move to higher ground—from race and color to content of character.

And here we were, just from delivering the demands of the right to vote campaign to governing powers in the nation's capital, delivering the benediction at the Inauguration of an African American as the forty-fourth president of these United States. What a mighty God we serve!

In the joy of this new beginning, we must not let anybody quench our spirits, nor dim our lights, nor mute our trumpets, nor silence our voices! We must not let them work harder, love more dearly, vote more faithfully! We must not let them turn back the clock. We have marched too long, prayed too hard, bled too profusely, and died too young to let anybody turn back the clock on our journey to justice! Even with a troubling economy, we have faith in a visionary leadership! "America! America! God shed His grace on thee, and crown thy good with brotherhood from sea to shining sea!" In the joy of a new beginning!

THE BEAT GOES ON

CHAPTER TWENTY-EIGHT

THE JOSEPH E. LOWERY INSTITUTE FOR JUSTICE AND HUMAN RIGHTS

The mission of the Institute is to provide a platform for citizens of every walk of life to learn the important principles that underlie nonviolent advocacy. Central to this mission is a push to provide future leaders and "change agents" with opportunities to explore the moral, ethical, and theological imperatives for justice and human rights for all people. *Simply put, our mission is to change lives for the better, in a real and permanent way.*

The Joseph E. Lowery Institute for Justice and Human Rights at Clark Atlanta University provides a forum for dialogue and a laboratory for the analysis of issues related to a variety of social inequity: Human Rights, Workers' Rights, Election Reform, Voting Rights, Anti-Poverty Measures, Economic Justice, Environmental Justice, Racism, and Sexism.

Our mentoring programs are equipping boys and girls to emerge as leaders and "Agents of Change" to make a difference in their communities and to create the Beloved Community of which Dr. King spoke and Dr. Lowery has encouraged through his message, "Let us turn *to* each other and not *on* each other."

Symposiums on the Criminal Justice System, Education, Economic and Financial Justice, and Nonviolence are ongoing outreach programs. The Institute is continuing a "Mission to Malawi" project, which seeks to educate teens and preteens in the United States and in Malawi about HIV/AIDS. Through mentoring, workshops, and bonding activities, these groups learn the facts and develop the confidence to make important lifestyle decisions.

Learn more at www.loweryinstitute.org.

PROFILING THE BLACK PRESENCE IN AMERICA

When I reflect on your genuine faith, which first dwelled in your grandmother Lois, and your mother Eunice, and now I am persuaded in you, therefore, stir up (rekindle, fan into flame) the gift of God, which is in you. For God did not give us the spirit of timidity, but of power, love and self-discipline.
—2 Timothy 1:5-7

You are a chosen people, a royal priesthood, extraordinary, a holy nation, a people belonging to God that you may declare the praises of him who called you out of the darkness into his marvelous light.
—1 Peter 2:9

It's vital to know where you've come from; if not, you won't know when somebody is taking you back.

Know who you are. Our theology is never static—it's deeply rooted but never restricted. God's revelation is a continuum. Knowing where we come from helps us understand how we got over, and knowing who we are shields us from accepting the definition of our enemies about who we are. We must define ourselves from Diop to Douglass to Dubois; Mandela to Martin; Truth to Tubman.

Our profile moves beyond individual achievements to congregational, institutional, and cultural deposits in the national bank, which produced interest and dividends on the national ledger.

A black presence demonstrated the power of the human spirit to translate adversity to opportunity. For God has given us a spirit of power to turn stumbling blocks into stepping-stones. Even if life hands us a lemon, we take the water of hope and the sugar of faith, we stir it and shake it well with determination before using, and we make lemonade.

We have overcome many barriers, we have come through many dangerous toils and snares: legal, psychological, political, social economic barriers; we have navigated treacherous seas, ridden turbulent airways, crossed raving rivers—with always one more river to cross.

Sometimes we've overcome with plain old mother wit from Lois and Eunice and sometimes with scholarly research like Diop, Douglass, Dubois, and Drew.

Sometimes with simple faith like my grandmother who worked as a domestic in the "big house" around the corner where they would not let her enter through the front door. Her black hands would knead white dough; her brown and black breast would feed hungry white mouths; but as a person she could not come in the front door. "What did you do, Ma Polly?" I asked. She answered, "Son, I would come in the back door as ordered and put on my work apron, take the broom and go out the front door onto the front porch without speaking to anyone in the house and sweep the front porch. When I finished sweeping, I would pull my shoulders back, hold my head high, open the front door, and as far as I was concerned that was the first time I had gone into the house that day."

The brand of power she used enabled us to move from slave ships to space ships, from log cabins to governors' mansions, and from the outhouse to the White House. The sour cord of discrimination was transposed into a symphony of agitation and determination where every round goes higher.

Individually, congregationally, and institutionally, we have demonstrated in unparalleled fashion and uncontradictable effectiveness what authentic patriotism is all about. We are living definitions of true patriotism. Not just because from Crispus Attucks to Colin Powell we have fought, bled, and died in every war, not just because a black person convicted of treason is as rare as a cotton patch in the North Pole, but because we have challenged a nation to honor the noble ideas of liberty and justice.

Authentic patriotism is not a bumper sticker that says, "Love it or leave it," but it is loving it so much that we won't leave it alone until it straightens up and flies right. As Barry White sang, "practice what you preach" by translating the Bill of Rights into righteous policies and just practices; into racial and gender inclusiveness; and into a movement which frees the oppressed and the oppressor as well. Our movement has spread beyond national boundaries from Selma to Soweto; Philadelphia to Peking; Tennessee to Tiananmen Square; and from Montgomery to Manila.

Finally, the profile of black presence must include the establishment of the efficacy and power of applying the moral imperatives of our faith to political, social, and economic problems. We have faith in a God who is faithful to us. Our power is best profiled when we opt for not what is political but what is *right*; not what is expedient but *right*; not what is popular but *right*. "Not by might, nor by power, but by my spirit," says the Lord (Zechariah 4:6).